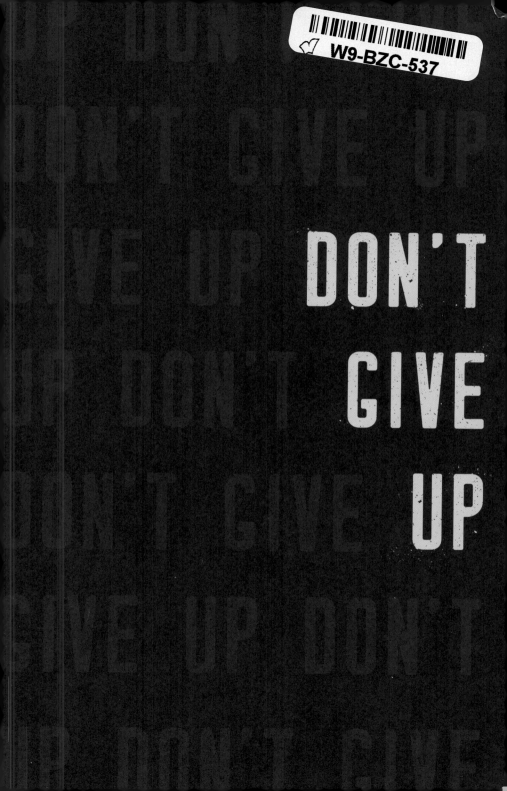

DON'T GIVE UP

"In *Don't Give Up*, Kyle Idleman gives us encouragement to keep believing, keep fighting, and keep perspective. If you need to find your courage and strength in the midst of life's challenges, this book is for you."

Dr. **Kevin Leman**, *New York Times* bestselling author of *Have a New Kid by Friday* and *The Birth Order Book*

"We've all faced moments in life (far too many) when we're tempted to stand down, give up, walk away. Yet Kyle Idleman heralds a powerful and personal call that the grip of grace never lets go—and neither should we. No. Matter. What. Fusing treasured insight with practical advice, *Don't Give Up* is a message we all need. Within these pages, you'll find what you need to stand tall, push forward, and experience the breakthrough God has for you."

Margaret Feinberg, author of *Taste and See: An Aspiring Foodie's Search for God among Butchers, Bakers, and Fresh Food Makers*

"As a Super Bowl–winning coach, NASCAR champion–owner, husband, father, leader, and average Joe, I have learned to dig deep, fight hard, and never give up. Read Kyle Idleman's *Don't Give Up* and find what it means to gain the God-given confidence and courage to keep going and finish strong."

Joe Gibbs, author of *Game Plan for Life*

"I once ran a marathon that had no crowd. No one cheering—until one guy, when I had about a mile to go, standing on a corner who said, 'Looking good, man! Keep going! You're almost there!' It meant the world to me. This book is that guy, all over again. I needed this. We all need this. Thank you, Kyle, for being real . . . and really, deeply encouraging."

Brant Hansen, author of *Unoffendable* and *Blessed Are the Misfits*

"In *Don't Give Up*, Kyle Idleman will teach you to listen to the crowd, throw off all that hinders, and run the race God has marked out for you. You will go forward with the courage to keep going no matter what comes your way."

Tamika Catchings, author of *Catch a Star*

"Finding courage when you are ready to quit is easier said than done. But Kyle Idleman encourages us to not give up—to gain the strength to continue on no matter what comes your way. *Don't Give Up* is just what you need to bring yourself into the life God meant for you."

Mike Cosper, author of *Recapturing the Wonder*

"Have you ever felt overwhelmed, beaten down, or ready to quit? Hold on and read *Don't Give Up*. In these pages, Kyle Idleman teaches us to be free from everything that hinders and all that entangles. Kyle teaches us how to draw strength from God so that we cannot just survive but thrive."

Jonathan "JP" Pokluda, author of *Welcome to Adulting*, director of The Porch, and teaching pastor at Watermark

"Kyle Idleman is one of the nation's leading Christian voices, which is why I read everything he writes. In *Don't Give Up* he confronts the wall of pain, loss, and rejection common to all, and teaches us how to acquire the courage to push through. *Don't Give Up* came just in time—every page has brilliant impact."

Bob Merritt, author of *Get Wise*

"Each of us faces a choice between stepping up to take agency in our own lives and sitting back while life happens to us. Kyle Idleman wants us to step up, and *Don't Give Up* could be just what you need to rouse yourself from complacency and spur yourself on to the life God intends you to live."

Michael Hyatt, bestselling author of *Your Best Year Ever*

"We all go through times as a leader, spouse, parent, or Jesus follower when life feels overwhelming and we want to throw in the towel and quit. It's during those times we need Kyle Idleman's *Don't Give Up* to help us find the God-given confidence and courage to keep going and finish strong."

Dave Ferguson, author of *Hero Maker*

Praise for Kyle Idleman

"Kyle is a brilliant, compassionate, and thoughtful communicator who presents the truth of Scripture in a fresh, relevant, and persuasive way."

Rick Warren, author of *The Purpose-Driven Life*

"Fresh, insightful, practical—Kyle's writing and teaching are helping countless people. I'm thrilled with how God is using him to challenge and encourage both Christians and those who are checking out the faith. Count me among his many fans!"

Lee Strobel, bestselling author of *The Case for Christ*

"Kyle knows where we live and where we could live with God's help. He is committed to helping us move in the right direction. If you need a helping hand in your journey, he'll point you to the right Person."

Max Lucado, bestselling author of *Unshakeable Hope*

"Kyle is a remarkable writer. As he opens his heart and God's Word, he shares stories that are both moving and meaningful, and he confesses his own weaknesses with stunning transparency."

Liz Curtis Higgs, bestselling author of *Bad Girls of the Bible*

"Kyle has a way of communicating grace that invites all people to partake. You will be challenged to receive God's love and mercy daily and freely give it to others."

Mark Batterson, *New York Times* bestselling author of *The Circle Maker*

"Kyle will challenge even the most obedient Christians to relook at their relationship with Christ."

Mike Huckabee, former Governor of Arkansas and bestselling author

DON'T GIVE UP

FAITH THAT GIVES YOU THE
CONFIDENCE TO KEEP BELIEVING AND
THE COURAGE TO KEEP GOING

KYLE IDLEMAN

BakerBooks
a division of Baker Publishing Group
Grand Rapids, Michigan

© 2019 by Kyle Idleman

Published by Baker Books
a division of Baker Publishing Group
PO Box 6287, Grand Rapids, MI 49516-6287
www.bakerbooks.com

Printed in the United States of America

Library of Congress Cataloging-in-Publication Data
Names: Idleman, Kyle, author.
Title: Don't give up : faith that gives you the confidence to keep believing and the courage to keep going / Kyle Idleman.
Description: Grand Rapids : Baker Publishing Group, 2019.
Identifiers: LCCN 2018043308 | ISBN 9780801019425 (pbk.)
Subjects: LCSH: Faith.
Classification: LCC BV4637 .I35 2019 | DDC 248.8/6—dc23
LC record available at https://lccn.loc.gov/2018043308

Some names and details have been changed to protect the privacy of the individuals involved.

Published in association with the literary agent Don Gates of The Gates Group, www.the-gates-group.com.

19 20 21 22 23 24 25   7 6 5 4 3 2 1

CONTENTS

INTRODUCTION

Let's imagine that you and I run into each other at some random everyday location. You can pick it. The waiting area of the auto shop, the departure gate of the airport, or the cereal aisle at the grocery store—where I begin our conversation by telling you the box of Apple Jacks in the cart is for my kids. We've only just met, and already our entire relationship is based on a lie.

In the course of our conversation I ask you how life is going and you give the instinctual response of "Fine," or "Pretty good," or "Can't complain." But I know that's not completely true. There are some things happening in your life that are difficult. Some things you would change if you could. I understand that you don't mention those things because it's not socially acceptable to respond to "How ya doing?" with an honest answer about your pain, struggles, and challenges.

But since this conversation isn't real and we are only imagining, let's imagine that it isn't culturally unacceptable and I really do want to know how you are doing. How would you respond? Instead of asking "How ya doing?" what if I asked "If there's one thing you would change in your life, what would it be?" I asked a few thousand people on social media this question and got all kinds of responses.

> Their grade school–age child is losing the battle with cancer. They're angry with God.
>
> They've been married less than two years. They're ready to call it quits.
>
> She's been sick for too long, and the doctors have no idea why.
>
> They love their special needs child, and they're also overwhelmed and discouraged.
>
> Another dud pregnancy test.
>
> Another screaming tantrum directed at the kids.
>
> Another game spent sitting on the bench.
>
> Another visit to the website he knows he must avoid.
>
> She feels invisible to her husband and kids.
>
> His aging father won't accept Christ.
>
> She sees a future of unending debt.
>
> He can't climb out of depression.
>
> She can't climb out of unemployment.
>
> He's certain no one will ever love him.

I could keep going, but you don't need me to. Chances are you've got your own story. A struggle that is just as real, just as glaring, as any of these. Whatever your story, my words of encouragement to you would probably be the same. They are the same words I need to hear on a regular basis.

Don't Give Up.

I could package it differently: *Keep going. Don't stop. Hang on. Hold fast. Stand firm.*

Hallmark has likely done a few hundred more variations on the theme, with the glossy sunrise and lighthouse images to go with them. Why? Because the need for these simple words of encouragement is universal.

Don't give up. Those three words offer more than comfort; they offer courage.

> Someone who is dealing with grief needs to hear it differently than someone who is struggling with guilt.
>
> Someone who is walking out needs to hear it differently than someone who is being walked out on.
>
> Someone who is angry needs to hear it differently than someone who is addicted.
>
> Someone who is scared needs to hear it differently than someone who is sick.
>
> Someone who is desperate needs to hear it differently than someone who is indifferent.

As a pastor I've discovered that some variation of "Don't give up" is the message most people need to hear, although I have found that my tone isn't always the same.

Sometimes I say it with a kind of gentle tone. Let's call it the Mister Rogers approach. Sometimes struggling people need to be comforted. That means a warm smile, a soft voice, and an awesome sweater jacket like Mister Rogers wore.

This kind of encouragement to not give up usually includes pats on the back and statements such as:

I'm so sorry for what you're going through.

You've been through so much. I don't know how you've kept going.

It's not fair, and it's not your fault.

Things are going to work out. You'll see.

People like to hear things like that. In fact, if you picked up this book because its title is *Don't Give Up*, then chances are these are the things you want me to say to you. But here's what I've realized. Sometimes, when we feel like giving up, what we *want* is Mister Rogers to come knock on our door—but what we *need* is William Wallace.

Who is William Wallace? You saw *Braveheart*, right? That's his story, and I don't remember him wearing any sky-blue sweater jackets or white tennis shoes. He's not a hug-it-out guy, telling you to cheer up. No, this guy paints his face like a hardcore football fan. He grabs you by the shoulder, and he says—even *growls*—stuff like this:

This is not the time to give up and go home!

It's time to fight!

Don't you dare back down!

You're tired. You're discouraged. But don't give up!

When we're right on the edge of quitting, when we're beaten down, when we feel utterly overwhelmed, comfort may sustain us but courage is often what we need to move forward. It gets us taking back the ground we've lost in the battle.

Let's call it by another name: *encouragement*. The New Oxford American Dictionary defines encouragement as "The action of giving someone support, confidence, or hope," which is pretty much what we think it means. Until we get to the secondary definition: "Persuasion to do or to continue something."[1]

That second one has verbs. Now we're getting somewhere.

Encouragement is a battle cry. It's a call to move, to act, to advance. What kind of words accomplish that? To encourage means, of course, to give courage—to "speak courage into." That's not the same as making someone feel better. It's not patching up a wound but rather putting a weapon in their hands. It's giving them a fresh horse and the will to advance.

I don't know which one you need. The blue sweater guy or the blue face guy. Probably a little bit of both. But I've discovered that many of us have some voices of comfort in our lives yet what we really need is a voice of courage. We may feel the need for sympathy when what we really need is strength.

Listen to the Crowd

I coached my son's basketball team. These were sixth and seventh graders. The season ended with a tournament. If we won the first game, we would play in the championship round on the same day.

We won that first game, but it took an overtime performance that exhausted the team. So there we were in the championship game, and you could tell our kids didn't have much gas left in their tanks, physically or emotionally. A couple of them had also been sick during the week, running temperatures, but they weren't about to miss the big game. And one of our guys kept cramping up, his first experience with that. We told him to put in a little more effort and the cramps would go away.

We got to the fourth quarter, and several kids were asking to sit out. But this was it—the final minutes of the season!

A cool plastic trophy was on the line. A trophy that looked identical to the runner-up trophy, and the participation trophy for that matter, but I still wanted it.

I wasn't the only minister coaching. One of the other guys was too, and he was more "ministerial" than me— compassionate, gentle, and gracious. He gathered the team around him during a time-out and said, "Hey, you guys have been doing great today. You've been fighting hard. I know you're tired. You've been giving it everything you've got."

So what were his next words? "You've done so well, take a seat on the bench. Chill and sip some water, guys." Nope. He's not *that* "ministerial."

Instead, he launched into a classic pep talk that, if filmed, would have entered the annals of classic, inspirational talks and been enshrined forever as "The Suck It Up Speech."

It began and ended with those three motivational words. He said something like this: "You guys need to suck it up! Suck. It. Up. You think nobody but you is tired? You've worked too hard to quit now. Get back out there right now and give it every ounce of what you've got! You can rest when the game is over, but *it's not over.* Stop complaining about being tired, suck it up, and let's WIN. THIS. THING."

I was watching the eyes of the boys and saw tiny little flames igniting. Their will to win was heating up. They stormed back on the court like sixth and seventh grade Huns sacking a village, and they won the championship.*

Those kids wanted recognition because they'd played hard. They needed encouragement to finish what they'd started.

---

* I have the plastic trophy to prove it. And a Dairy Queen coupon that has since expired.

The Bible is filled with passages that speak courage into our lives, but one in particular has always held special power for me. I'm talking about the first three verses in Hebrews 12. This passage challenges us not to grow weary or give up.

> Therefore, since we are surrounded by such a great cloud of witnesses, let us throw off everything that hinders and the sin that so easily entangles. And let us run with perseverance the race marked out for us, fixing our eyes on Jesus, the pioneer and perfecter of faith. For the joy set before him he endured the cross, scorning its shame, and sat down at the right hand of the throne of God. Consider him who endured such opposition from sinners, so that you will not grow weary and lose heart. (Heb. 12:1–3)

We're not certain exactly who wrote Hebrews, but its audience is pretty clear: people who are weary; people who are losing heart. In other words, everybody. On any number of occasions. This writer wants to speak courage into readers' souls.

Let's start at the beginning of verse 1: "Therefore, since we are surrounded by such a great cloud of witnesses . . ."

In just a few words, he not only urges us not to give up but points us to a source of motivation, a source of inspiration, and a source of accountability. He calls that last one a "cloud of witnesses." What in the world (or out of it) is that?

The clue is in the word *therefore*, which points us back to the previous chapter. Hebrews 11 is sometimes called "The Faith Hall of Fame." It offers a list of people who faced enormous challenges yet found the faith to keep believing and the courage to keep fighting.

So those are the witnesses. But what's this about a cloud? Two different words are used for "cloud" in the New Testament. One is a single, detached, distinct mass of whiteness you see in the sky. The other—the word used here—is something wider and more powerful. It's an *encompassing* cloud, more like a heavy fog that surrounds us. You look up in the sky and see the first one. You *feel* the second one, around and enveloping you.

The ancient Greeks used that second kind of cloud to describe a crowd, a massive gathering of people. So in Hebrews 12 we have the idea of a huge throng of people all around us, wherever we go.

There's a psychological phenomenon called *pareidolia*, the mind's ability to see an image when there is none. An example is when somebody sees the face of the Virgin Mary on a grilled cheese sandwich.* The most common pareidolia experience is when we see pictures in the clouds. So when you read about the faith heroes in Hebrews 11, think of them as faces in the cloud of tough issues that make up life.

Someone Who Sees

How does the cloud of witnesses help us to keep going, continue pushing on, and refuse to give up?

Let's look at another word: *witnesses*. A witness could be someone who sees something. An eyewitness observes something happening.

Because of that meaning, some people read Hebrews 12 and think the "cloud of witnesses" is watching in heaven

---

* That sandwich sold for $28,000. Maybe it would have been more if the bread had been organic multigrain.

as we go about our lives. I'm initially skeptical about that, because I understand these past heroes to be living in heaven, a place of perfect peace and joy. I'm not sure they'd be fully experiencing that by spending their time watching us struggle.

On the other hand, that meaning of *witness* could make sense if thought of in a certain way. What if these heroes were caught up in a heavenly kind of joy rather than an earthly one? For example, some scholars argue that the joy of heaven isn't found in avoiding what happens here on earth but in having a full, eternal perspective of what it *means*. They understand that we're moving toward our greatest blessings when we fight through our toughest trials.

So are those heroes sitting in the stands of heaven, watching us run the race? I have to say that's a possible interpretation of this phrase, and it can work. The Living Bible thinks so. It paraphrases Hebrews 12:1 this way:

Since we have such a huge crowd of men of faith watching us from the grandstands . . .

The language may be figurative or literal, but if we define witnesses as "those who see," we're invited to enjoy a powerful, inspiring idea: the applause of history's greatest heroes at the very time we feel the loneliest and most overwhelmed—shouts of encouragement from Jacob and Joseph and Moses and David.*

Reach for that mental picture the next time you feel discouraged and ready to quit. There are throngs of achievers who have gone before you, felt exactly as you feel, and

* I imagine Moses as the one yelling, "Suck it up!"

somehow got back in the game and won the trophy. You are anything but alone.

Play that highlight tape found in Hebrews 11. Reread the stories of those heroes and think about how they persevered. What gave them the power to endure? And remember, as you're watching their highlights, they're watching yours.

A friend of mine told me about the moment he almost gave up while running the Derby Marathon in Louisville, Kentucky.* The course took my friend through a park notorious for its hills. As he was coming out of the park, on the back end of the race, his legs felt dead. He had an overwhelming urge to give in to fatigue—when suddenly the route took him right past one of his friends, standing out on the road to cheer him on. My friend had an immediate awareness of accountability. It wasn't just some unknown spectator watching but someone whose face he recognized and whose voice he knew. He found new energy to finish.

In the moments of life where we feel exhausted and are struggling to keep going, it makes a difference to hear those voices from the Scriptures, a cloud of witnesses who are alive and counting on us.

Someone Who Says

So that's one kind of witness: someone who sees something. But there's another possibility. It also means someone who *says* something. That's what we mean when we speak of someone "bearing witness." Not only did they see it but they

* I have to tell my friend's story about running a marathon, since I have no marathon stories of my own to tell. It turns out that marathon stories actually require running marathons.

also testify to it. They're witnesses to the truth. Looking at the Hebrews example, this makes sense too. The heroes of faith bear testimony in the pages of Scripture.

But which meaning did the writer intend? Five times this word for *witness* is used in Hebrews 11, and on each occasion the context points to *saying* rather than seeing. Hebrews 11:4 is the key example. The writer is telling us about Abel, the son of Adam and Eve. What got Abel inducted into the Faith Hall of Fame? The offerings he gave to God. Hebrews 11:4 tells us that Abel still speaks, even though he is dead. So it's all about his bearing witness for us; speaking to us, even from beyond the grave.

Abel and all the other heroes continue to tell their stories, across time and eternity, whenever we're tired, weary, and ready to check out. They keep on speaking, and every word they say is about pushing on, getting that victory. It's never, "Hey, you've done great. Nobody's going to blame you for packing it in."

In this first section of this book, "Listen to the Crowd," I want us to get that message and a whole lot more. These witnesses do not just pump their fists and cheer. They have real words of power to speak into our struggles. Sometimes their words may not be the ones we wish for at that moment. But they're always the ones we need.

Get ready to take a stroll through the Hall of Fame. We're going to look at the lives of a few of those who have been uploaded to the cloud of witnesses. I hope you'll be inspired enough to learn even more about each of the other characters, because their messages never grow old.

When you feel like giving up, listen for the crowd.

1

Keep Believing

Have you ever tried to put together a puzzle without the box?

When I was growing up, we would go visit my grandparents. This was before the days of cell phones and iPads, and there was never much to do at their house. I had to annoy my sisters and cousins for entertainment.

Then after a few days, absolutely desperate, I'd get out one of my grandmother's puzzles. The catch: most of her puzzles weren't kept in the box they came in. She had large ziplock bags, each containing a different puzzle.*

I'd pour hundreds of puzzle pieces out of the bag and onto the floor, and turn each of them over, wondering what kind of picture they might form. Maybe it was a skyline of Chicago, or an old farmhouse in a field, or three snobby cats. I had no idea. Just for the irony, I'd like to think one of the puzzles was a picture of a frustrated grandson trying to put

---

* I never asked her why, but I assume it had something to do with the Great Depression. That was her go-to answer for all of our questions.

together a puzzle without the box. Who knows what they pictured, because I never finished a ziplock puzzle. I'd get the edges done, maybe connect a few easy pieces, then I'd get frustrated and zip it back up.

When you have a few pieces but no big picture, it's easy to give up.

The big picture is your guide for the whole process. It shows you where you're going. It assures you that everything interlocks in a way that makes sense.

The writer of Hebrews 11 defines the big picture of the cloud of witnesses as *faith*. Faith is the principle that joins all these various lives. Here's how the writer puts it:

> Now faith is confidence in what we hope for and assurance about what we do not see. This is what the ancients were commended for. (Heb. 11:1–2)

Faith is a confidence that keeps believing all the pieces are going to somehow fit together, even when you don't have the big picture to work from. It's believing that God has a purpose, even when there seems to be no reason.

Pastors visit church members who are in the hospital for different reasons. But in reality, you don't want to see me walk into your hospital room. If it's me, that's a sure sign it's something serious. We have staff pastors who make visits, and I'm only called upon when the situation is grave. If you have your tonsils removed, then wake up to find me sitting there, something terrible happened during your tonsillectomy.

But the fact that my visits tend to correspond with tragedy means that I get to see how neatly faith fits into the picture at the very times when life doesn't seem to make sense.

One night I was called to the hospital to visit a young couple. The young lady was going into labor with their first child, whom they'd already named Lilly. Friends and family were there and ready to celebrate. But when the time for delivery came, the nurse couldn't find a heartbeat. The doctor brought the heartbreaking news that Lilly had died and would have to be delivered as a stillborn baby.

I walked into a situation of grief and weeping, and heard cries of despair. I stood with the family, surrounding the bed, to mourn with that mother, until someone pointed me to a room next door. There sat the father in a rocking chair, holding the lifeless body of his baby girl. His tears fell on the pink blanket specially knitted for her.

Sometimes the best thing you can say is nothing at all. You simply sit quietly with those who suffer, and you share their grief. I did that, praying silently for this family. After a few minutes, the father took a deep breath and said something startling: "I guess this is when I find out if I really believe what I say I believe."

Again, all I could do was nod and keep praying. Finally I knelt beside the rocker, placed a hand on his shoulder, and began to pray for him aloud. A few sentences in, I heard singing coming from the other room, where the family and friends surrounded the mother. I broke off my prayer and listened: "How great is our God, sing with me. . . . How great, how great is our God."[1]

They didn't know the verses, so they sang the chorus through again and again, each time a tiny bit louder than the last. Their confidence in those words grew stronger, more insistent. I decided to sneak away and give the family some time together. As I moved down the hall, the singing continued. Three nurses stood in the hallway listening—silent, respectful, overcome.

There are moments when you find out if you really believe what you say you believe. Faith, at such times, is confidence the picture is there, even though it looks like chaos.

Another college application rejected.

Another job interview with no callback.

Another relationship with no proposal.

Another doctor's appointment with no diagnosis.

Faith carries through.

Off the Map

Abraham is one of the first witnesses in Hebrews 11. God's plan was to build a nation from which the Messiah would eventually be born, to save the world from sin. God chose a man named Abram, who would later be called Abraham, to be the father of this great nation. Abraham's story is recorded for us in the Old Testament, but he's also mentioned some seventy-five times in the New Testament. Here's what we're told about him in Hebrews 11:

> By faith Abraham, when called to go to a place he would later receive as his inheritance, obeyed and went, even though he did not know where he was going. (v. 8)

The full story is found in Genesis 12. Abraham is told to leave his homeland, but God doesn't reveal the final destination. Abraham and his wife, Sarah, live in Harran, a city close to the border of what is now Turkey and Syria.

Harran is where they're comfortable. Life there is predictable and safe. Abraham and Sarah have a plan, a big picture of their future—and it's in Harran.

Then, suddenly, God shows up and tells Abraham to move. God's big picture is a whole different landscape, and it's not as pretty. It's actually not a picture at all but a lot of strange pieces yet to come together. This is a plan that requires faith.

Faith for Abraham means more than leaving what he knows; it's about moving away without even knowing the destination. Imagine the weight of that, the courage required. Maybe the conversation between the couple sounded something like this:

> "Honey, I just heard from the Lord. He wants us to move."
> "Seriously? We've lived here all our lives! Where are we supposed to go?"
> "Well, God didn't mention anything about that. Anyway, the U-Haul is out front, ready to load up."
> "Wait. What you're saying is, we're moving but we don't know where? Why would we do that? Because we're crazy?"
> "Because we believe God."
> "Which one?"

Hold on—which one?

Here you have to understand that Abraham didn't have a Sunday school education. He had no sermons to hear, no hymns to sing—he didn't grow up with any knowledge of God whatsoever. There was no Israel, no chosen people; he was part of a pagan family. Joshua 24 tells us that Terah, Abraham's father, was an idol worshiper. Many of us are familiar with the idea that there is one God who keeps his promises and is a loving Father beyond anything we could imagine. Abraham had never heard the first word about any of that.

Imagine growing up in a home without parents of strong, resilient faith. Maybe that's just what you did.

Consider a child growing up and seeing his parents going through life without a fixed view of how things work; moving from one strategy to another, maybe praying to different gods all the time.

Now God shows up to a grown-up Abraham with a really big ask: *Pack up everything you own and start walking; I'll say when to stop.*

Abraham's response: "So Abram went . . ." (Gen. 12:4).

He has faith to move forward—even if it doesn't make sense. He doesn't decide to quit on the puzzle just because he isn't given the big picture.

We don't like uncertainty; we're taught that it's foolish to walk into the unknown. Therefore we have a tendency to give up if there's no clear map or GPS. But faith that endures has confidence that even when we don't know where we're going, God does.

We do our traveling while trusting in a satellite in the sky that speaks to a computer in our cars. The directions come step by step, turn by turn, with plenty of advance notice. No thinking is required, really. The pleasant voice says, "Turn right here." And that's just the way we like it.

Think about times in your own life when you wanted more details—stress-free movement. Life never works that way, for anyone.

Not during the monthly heartbreaking event for the couple who only ever see the negative symbol at the end of their pregnancy test. Not for the fully invested employee, working hard for that first big break—only to keep getting pats on the back rather than the promotion she deserves. Not for those in their late thirties, still waiting to find that special someone who never arrives. No satellite relays our next turn in the things that matter most.

Life's detours are undeniably bumpy, confusing, and longer than we anticipate. However, just like actual detours on the road, once we've arrived at our destination, those detours can start to make sense. Or sometimes they don't, but we decide that's all right. Because the joy of finally arriving where we've yearned to be has put the detours in perspective, even if we don't understand them.

Risky Faith

The courageous faith of Abraham and Sarah requires risk-taking. There are no great stories of a faith that was risk-free. Risk-dodging can be a way of giving up before the journey even begins. Yet there's a hidden irony: playing it safe turns out to be the greatest risk you can take. The lives of the faith heroes tell us that.

Larry Laudan, a philosopher of science, has spent the last decade studying risk management. He writes of how we live in a society so fear-driven that we suffer from what he calls "risk-lock," a condition like gridlock that leaves us unable to do anything or go anywhere. He has concluded that, as much as we try and avoid risks, the truth is that *everything involves risk.*[2] "Risk-free" is a myth.

No matter where you go or how safe you play it, risk is waiting for you. My recliner at home carries certain health hazards. My remote control has doubled, at times, as a dangerous weapon. Sometimes I sense God calling me out of the house, but reclining and flipping through channels, usually over a bowl of Apple Jacks, keeps me glued to my seat. God has called me to be a husband, father, and pastor, yet I could waste a lot of time vegging out in front of the TV screen. That's a risk I face on a daily basis.

Giving up and giving in to the temptation to check out of my responsibilities is the most dangerous risk of all. Funny how it seems so safe . . .

Abraham planned on a low-risk future—kicking up his feet in Harran; living the way his father did, and his father before him; having no particular god who made demands. But faith doesn't tend to be sedentary. It's always sending us somewhere.

Here are the questions I find myself wrestling with:

Am I following God in a way that requires faith?

Do I do anything at all in my life that requires courage and confidence?

Let me direct those same questions to you. Instead of asking if you have given up or quit, let me ask if you are doing anything in your life that requires courage and confidence. If your answer is yes, then I have a follow-up question for you: Can you tell me a story?

Risking faith, the kind of courageous faith we see in Abraham, always has a story attached to it.

Hebrews 11 helps us understand faith not by giving a long, theological explanation but by giving us names and stories.

Don't tell me you have faith; tell me a story.

A story of faith is almost always a "don't give up" story of perseverance. A story of pushing through and refusing to put the puzzle away even when the picture isn't clear. The tendency is to feel sorry for ourselves and to dwell on our unfair circumstances. But faith that doesn't quit means taking action and moving forward. It's a determination to act on what needs to happen rather than dwelling on how something happened. Like Abraham's story, all stories of faith reach an intersection where a decision must be made between staying put and playing it safe or taking a risk and moving forward. Can you tell me a story about a time in your life when you found yourself at the intersection and kept going?

Against All Hope

By the time we get to Genesis 15, a lot of time has passed by, and Abraham and Sarah still haven't had any children. God has been sketchy in the details, but he was very clear on the children part. The couple wouldn't forget something like that.

But years pass, and nothing. They must be starting to doubt. Maybe they've heard God wrong. Maybe this God forgot the whole thing. But actually, he repeats his promise.

> He took him outside and said, "Look up at the sky and count the stars—if indeed you can count them." Then he said to him, "So shall your offspring be." (Gen. 15:5)

It sounds terrific—really it does. But there's a nagging problem: Abraham and Sarah are an elderly, barren couple. Hebrews 11 tells us Sarah was way "past childbearing age" and Abraham was "as good as dead." I'm no doctor, but "as good as dead" doesn't sound like a great qualification for fathering. Sarah's biological clock was blinking "12:00, 12:00."*

Month after month, year after year, this couple has tried to start a family, and nothing has happened. At some point, enough of nothing causes us to lose hope for some kind of something. And it's not as if God's promise ever made sense in the first place. But here's how Abraham responds to what God promised:

Abram believed the LORD . . . (v. 6)

Believed based on what? Nothing in this world—only faith itself.

For most people, this is where the puzzle pieces would go back in the bag. Even the edge pieces don't fit. Too much blue sky, not enough of a path. But Abraham keeps believing. Another New Testament passage, Romans 4, explains that it's this stubborn faith that allows him to persevere and not give up.

Against all hope, Abraham in hope believed and so became the father of many nations, just as it had been said to him, "So shall your offspring be." Without weakening in his faith, he faced the fact that his body was as good as dead—since he was about a hundred years old—and that Sarah's womb was also dead. Yet he did not waver through unbelief regarding the promise of God, but was strengthened in his faith and gave glory to God, being fully persuaded that God had power to do what he had promised. (Rom. 4:18–21)

"Against all hope." That would make a pretty good movie title. When all hope seemed lost, Abraham didn't give up.

* VCR reference. Ask your parents.

That phrase also reminds me of my friend Colleen McKain—a modern hero of the faith. She can tell a story of faith that doesn't quit, and I asked her to do just that, in her own words.

Chris and I married young. We both loved Jesus and each other, but after twenty years of marriage, we began having deep conflict. We tried to muddle through. We tried to keep up appearances. But things kept getting worse.

In our twenty-third year, he told me he'd had an affair, which he ended at that time. We moved forward, trying to hold things together for the sake of our family and because it seemed like the "right thing to do." Over the next four years, he had three additional affairs.

When I began to find out about those affairs, I was completely finished with him and our marriage. There was no hope for us. Because I'd had suspicions over the four years, I'd secretly made plans for my future without him. I'd saved money and acquired my own credit.

I was through and I had a reason to be. No one would blame me. In fact, anyone who knew felt sorry for me. Everyone I talked to seemed to agree that the marriage was beyond hope. I felt sure that my life would go on without him in the picture, and honestly, I was glad.

Early in the morning, on the day I found out about the final affair, God showed me a verse: 1 Samuel 12:16. "Now then, stand still and see this great thing the LORD is about to do before your eyes!"

I felt something I didn't even want to feel. I felt *hope*. Over the next few days, this verse kept coming back to mind. I was furious and full of rage toward my husband. But in the middle of the fury, that verse would come to mind. "Stand still and see this great thing the LORD is about to do before your eyes!"

I finally told God I'd watch and see what he might do, though I doubted he'd come through. After all, he hadn't answered my prayers for our marriage up to this point.

I began watching Chris like a hawk, keeping my end of the bargain to "watch what God might do." To my surprise, Chris began changing. Because of our history together, I could tell that these changes were real. I could tell this time was different. I began seeing things in his life that I had prayed over him for many years, and I knew this was only happening by God's intervention. I may have been ready to give up, but God was just getting started.

God gave me the faith to keep believing. My belief wasn't in Chris or myself, but I reached a place where I believed that God was going to save our marriage. Once I really believed that, I was all in.

The healing process was not easy. It included heated conversations, intense counseling, and deep reliance on the Lord. It brought to light things in both of our lives that needed to be addressed. From the world's wisdom and my own perspective, I'd have given up on our marriage. But God had a different plan. I now have a husband with a new heart, and in the process I have been made new too.

I don't know your story. I don't know what you've done or what's been done to you. I don't know what words have been spoken or what kind of betrayal has taken place. There's a lot I don't know, but I do know that God is able to do a great thing before your eyes, so hang on to that hope. Stay the course. Wait and see what he will do. Don't give up.

Redefining Faith

Faith that gives you the confidence to keep believing and the courage to keep going is not faith in life's circumstances; it's faith in God's character.

Sometimes faith does heal. Sometimes it does pay the bills. But sometimes what it gives you instead is something more precious: the strength to get through the day where there is no perfect healing, or when you're not sure how the bills are going to get paid.

Sometimes faith looks like a wife on her knees in a waiting room, praying for her husband who is in surgery for a tumor to be removed. The doctor comes in and says, "There is no tumor. We don't know what happened to it; it's just not there. We can't explain it."

Sometimes that's what faith looks like. But sometimes faith is a wife sitting in a cemetery and watching the casket of her husband being lowered into the ground. That's faith, too, you know. I've seen examples of both, and God was present in each.

Sometimes faith is a high school student who decides to start a Bible study on campus with no idea how it will go over. Incredibly, it just takes off. Wonderful, uplifting things are accomplished, and revival breaks out in the school.

Sometimes faith is a high school student who walks into school with a Bible. But she's mocked and ridiculed, and she spends four years of her life overlooked and misunderstood. That's faith too.

Sometimes faith is walking into the boss's office and telling him you refuse to lie or to mislead a client because of your convictions—and it ends up getting you a promotion. Sometimes the same faith will land you in the unemployment line.

Our faith is in God and the big picture that we won't completely see this side of eternity. It isn't easily—or rarely at all—measured by earthly success, but it's what keeps us aligned with the truth that sings out in our soul.

It's faith that keeps believing, even when the pieces don't seem to fit together.

Happily Never After

For Abraham and Sarah, it actually happens. It seems to take forever, but it happens. A child is born.

Sarah becomes pregnant, non-ticking biological clock and all. Abraham is beaming with pride, though "as good as dead." They have a baby son by the name of Isaac. They believed and persevered and hung on to their faith for years, and it was hard, but they got their reward. And lived happily ever after.

Until they didn't.

> Some time later God tested Abraham. He said to him, "Abraham!"
>
> "Here I am," he replied.
>
> Then God said, "Take your son, your only son, whom you love—Isaac—and go to the region of Moriah. Sacrifice him there as a burnt offering on a mountain I will show you." (Gen. 22:1–2)

There is no instance in the Bible of God ever requiring a human sacrifice. In fact, in several passages of Deuteronomy, God clearly condemns such practices. So this is off-brand for God. You and I as readers are tipped off about the truth in the first verse: "God tested Abraham."

But Abraham isn't given that heads-up. God simply tells him to take that son—the deepest, fiercest hope and dream of all his long life, the object of his adoration and Sarah's—and offer him up.

How is Abraham going to react? Here's how the next verse begins:

Early the next morning . . . (v. 3)

No questions, no second-guessing, no objections are recorded. Abraham waits for morning, then heads to Mount Moriah with his son and a sharp knife.

He *has* to have questions; it's basic humanity.

Why my son? It makes no sense. I'm to be the father of a great nation and you want me to kill my only son? And why all the way to Moriah? What's so significant about that place?

It will be a long walk, full of dread and the beginnings of grief. Every step offers the temptation, almost unbearable, to turn back. But whatever Abraham's private thoughts, his body acts out his obedience. He takes a few servants with him, and after a few days of travel, they get to Moriah. Abraham says to his servants, "Stay here with the donkey while I and the boy go over there. We will worship and then we will come back to you" (v. 5).

Did you catch that? The word *we*? Abraham says to the servants that "we will come back to you." He is obeying God, but it seems that even now, Abraham believes that Isaac will be spared. He's holding on to God's promise, and he keeps right on believing even when the story doesn't make sense. Faith peeks through at us in that verse.

Abraham knows that even though he has the puzzle pieces, he can't see the picture. He finds the courage to keep believing because he has confidence that God *does* have that picture, that he creates beautiful pictures, that he is worthy of trust.

Hebrews explains it this way: "Abraham reasoned that God could even raise the dead" (Heb. 11:19).

That is the kind of faith that keeps us from being discouraged and defeated. When things don't seem to be going as planned, and everything is falling apart, we have a stance: *God is able to make this work.* He's able to bring to life what is dead.

The question raised is this: Where is the point at which you would abandon all hope? For Abraham, it was somewhere on the other side of a command to

Give.

Up.

His.

Child.

Think on that . . . Abraham's limit is undefined. His hope in God knows no bounds. We have to figure maybe there isn't a limit; maybe it's possible to have an all-encompassing hope, because if God is powerful enough to raise the dead, what *can't* he do? And if you believe he is perfectly loving, what *won't* he do?

God tested to see if Abraham's red line of despair would be revealed. What would that test show with you? How far would your faith extend?

All-encompassing hope powers a faith that keeps on pushing, never gives up, always believes in God's intent.

The Big Picture

You probably know what happens next in the story of Abraham and Isaac. They reach the place God has described, and Abraham builds an altar to sacrifice his only son. But just as he raises his knife, an angel stops him and tells him not to lay a hand on the boy.

Abraham looks up and sees a ram caught by its horns in a thicket. He offers the ram as a sacrifice on the mountain instead of his son, and he names the place "The LORD Will Provide" (Gen. 22:14).

But even now, Abraham doesn't see the whole picture. In fact, the bigger picture won't come into focus for a few thousand years.

See, Abraham now lives in Beersheba, which is a small oasis in the southern desert. He has traveled three days to a place called Moriah. At the time, there isn't much there. But after a couple thousand years, the story comes to us of another Father who sacrifices his only Son. Only this time, there's no test. This is not a drill. God gives up his precious, perfect Son because of the precious, imperfect children he loves.

Over the years, a city called Jerusalem has risen nearby. Jesus is crucified on one of the hills once known as Mount Moriah. We don't know exactly which hill, but I bet we can guess.

The story of Abraham took place a few thousand years before the birth of Christ. We now live a few thousand years on the other side of his birth. And *still* the picture isn't complete. There are still puzzle pieces that God hasn't pushed neatly into place yet.

Your story is one of those pieces, so keep believing. Are you a little unsure about that? If the pieces of your life don't seem as if they could possibly fit into a beautiful picture, Abraham has a message for you from the cloud. It might go something like this: "I get it. Life hasn't measured up to your expectations. You're not alone; it's true for everyone—it certainly was for me. I thought there was a plan, and I waited and waited. I got older and older, until Sarah and I were scratching our heads. But I hung on.

"If you're feeling disappointed and disillusioned, keep believing. If you are confused and wondering if you somehow missed God's plan, keep believing. If you have done things your own way and only made things worse, keep believing. There *is* a picture. You can't see it now, but up here in the cloud, we have an incredible view. The picture is worth fitting into, and it's coming together, piece by piece. You're going to like it. That we promise.

"Keep believing! Don't give up!"

2

Keep Fighting

Deep Down Dark is one of the most gripping books I've ever read.[1] It tells the true story of the thirty-three miners in Chile who were trapped underground for sixty-nine days in 2010.

The stone that sealed them off was twice the size of the Empire State Building. There was no way for them to get to the surface, and a rescue seemed impossible. Any attempt to drill would likely cause a cave-in. One report put the chances of rescue and survival at 2 percent.

These thirty-three miners knew their situation was dire. It appeared they had virtually no chance of getting out alive, so they began to do what people do in the deep down dark: they thought about their lives.

They thought about the people they loved. They thought about their decisions and what they would've done differently. And, of course, they couldn't help but think about what would happen to them when they died. These are the things people reflect upon in the deep down dark.

One of the miners was José Enriquez. He was fifty-four years old and had been mining since the 1970s. The others knew he was a follower of Jesus, so they asked him if he would pray for them. He said yes, but on one condition. He liked to pray on his knees, as a way to humble himself before God. If he was to pray for them, he would appreciate their doing the same. The miners gathered around him, knelt, and closed their eyes.

José began to pray. "We aren't the best of men, but Lord, have pity on us," he began. "We are sinners. We need you to take charge of this situation." José made it clear to God that the men were desperate and that God was their only hope.

After he finished his prayer, the men asked him what they should do now. José told them they needed to confess their sins out loud. So they began doing that.

One man confessed his alcoholism. He looked back on what it had cost his family. Another confessed that he had trouble controlling his temper. One man confessed that he had not been a good father to his young daughter.

One after another, each man looked back on his life and repented the path that had led him to that place in his life. In true desperation, they cried out to God, and God—as he will often do—showed up.

Day after day, as they were stuck down there, José told them more about Jesus. There was no light, so his voice resonated in the dark. He could only preach from the Bible verses found in his memory banks. The men hung on to every word. They prayed from the soul, worshiped with their spirit, and cried out to God for help. They promised God that if he would rescue them from the terror of this cave, they would make changes and live their lives differently.

Desperate Moments

In a moment of desperation, when you feel like there is no hope, will you give up or will you cry out to God for help?

There is something about a desperate moment—a cold, pitch-black moment when all hope seems lost—that causes us to call out God's name in distress. In that moment of desperation, when you feel like things are out of your control and there is nothing you can do, there is a profound opportunity.

In his book *This Sickness Unto Death*, Danish philosopher Søren Kierkegaard speaks of moments of despair as having a remarkable silver lining.[2] In those moments, you are left with nothing to cling to, and you can only hope in something outside of yourself. You can discover God's power and presence in a way you've never experienced before.

The point of defeat—the urge to throw up your hands and surrender—seems like the most desolate corner of creation. It actually places you in prime position to experience God's strength and provision because, as it turns out, God is drawn to the desperate. If you trace this idea in Scripture, you'll find that God's deliverance often follows closely upon a time of desperation. His blessing tends to fall upon a condition of brokenness. Throughout history, his most powerful servants have all come from a place of desolation and defeat.

If you find yourself in the deep down dark, this is not the time to give up. Take your eyes off the door that has closed and look to the window that has opened. That's where the light of heaven rushes in. This is the time to keep fighting and crying out to God to rescue you. When you hear words like "Stage four," or "I don't love you anymore," or "We're downsizing," your every impulse might be to give up. But the cloud of witnesses is urging you to go against the grain and keep fighting.

It might be your day to meet God.

That's what happens to Jacob. Jacob is another "face in the cloud"—a figure from the roster of powerful faith witnesses in Hebrews 11. In the last chapter, we learned about Abraham and his son Isaac. Jacob is Isaac's son, Abraham's grandson.

There is an extraordinary story in the Old Testament of the time Jacob wrestled with the angel of the Lord. He literally did hand-to-hand combat with a supernatural being. The whole match is unlikely: the angel because, well, he's an angel; Jacob because fighting was never his thing.

We know that in stressful situations, people have the impulses of fight, flight, or freeze. Fighters strike back when confronted. Flyers take off; they run in the opposite direction. And others take the deer-in-the-headlights approach—they're paralyzed by fear.

Jacob was one to flee. We find him in the Scriptures in one bad situation after another, always of his own making, and he always hits the road. Esau, his brother, was the fighter.

That makes Jacob just like most people. There are always fighters and freezers, but flight is the most common response to fear. When talking about our fears, we're more comfortable talking about the unlikely physical threats we might face than admitting what really keeps us up at night. I'd rather tell you about spiders freaking me out than my fear of rejection. I would prefer to talk about my fear of tornadoes rather than tell a tableful of peers about my fear of inadequacy. But when I lie in the dark and worry—it's not about spiders or tornadoes. It's about measuring up, letting others down, missing my best.

Most of us have fears we'd rather not discuss. We fear coming into a responsibility and not being good enough: inadequacy. *What if something's wrong with me? What if I'm broken—not as smart? Not as beautiful? Not as funny or capable?* Rather than have that exposed, we run away.

We fear rejection and keep our friends at arm's length. Even a spouse may not be allowed to get too close. But it's really a form of running away.

We fear failure, so we don't apply for the promotion or try out for the team or ask the girl on a date. But what are we really doing? Fleeing.

Thinking about how fear makes us flee, I came up with a pitch for if I ever make it on *Shark Tank*. If you're not familiar with the show, inventors and entrepreneurs pitch their ideas to pretentious people who either shoot them down or invest in them.

Here's my latest idea: a soundtrack to make runners run faster. There are plenty of playlists out to help you push harder during a workout. Music with a fast beat will get your adrenaline going and push you to pick up the pace. But my invention is a little different. Each track would leverage a deep-seated fear to get you to run even faster. Here are few examples of possible tracks:

Track 1: "Zombie Apocalypse." Push *play* and you hear the moaning of zombies, growing louder as they get closer. You will instinctively run faster.

Track 2: "Mother-in-Law."* You know that voice. This one syncs up with your Fitbit and monitors your heart rate, and if you slow down, you can hear her voice approaching.

I figure I'd hit it big with this idea, because we all make tracks when the thing we fear is gaining on us. When what we fear is fast approaching, the most natural response is to give up and run in the opposite direction.

Run Away

Jacob's twin brother, Esau, was the fighter. Esau was technically the oldest. They may have been twins, but they were very different. Genesis 25:27 tells us that Esau hunted and loved the outdoors, but Jacob preferred staying inside. We can imagine Esau bringing home the dinner he hunted, and Jacob watching the cooking channel to find a recipe for it.

Take a guess which son Isaac, their father, liked best. Dad favored his outdoorsy son, while Rebekah, the mom, doted on Jacob. Every indication is that, in Jacob, we have the Bible's first mama's boy.

It was a classic case of brain versus brawn. Esau could have destroyed his barely younger brother in a fight, but Jacob had a way of outwitting him and escaping calamity. His great skill was manipulating situations to his advantage. As a matter of fact, his name means *grabber, deceiver, conniver, coercer*.

The first great example comes as Jacob cons Esau out of his birthright. Jacob has grown up hearing about Grandfather Abraham and God's blessing on him. That blessing

---

* To really get going, skip ahead to the last track, "Mother-in-Law Zombie Apocalypse."

and its birthright have passed to Isaac and will now go to Esau, who beat his brother to the birth canal in a thrilling finish. As the eldest, Esau has dibs on all the stuff that matters.

Jacob won't forget that, and he connives to get these things for himself. First, he talks his brother out of that birthright in a trade for a bowl of stew—Esau comes in from the fields, famished, and at that moment a hearty meal now seems better than a birthright later.

Then Jacob pulls another scam. He has the birthright, but in this culture, the paternal blessing is also incredibly important. It's a ritual in which the father lays hands on the son who is to carry on his legacy. Knowing his dad is old and going blind, he poses as Esau to take advantage of that ritual. He even puts goat's hair on his arms so that Isaac will reach out and think he's feeling the hairy biceps of his oldest son. Jacob makes it all work.

Now Jacob has both the birthright—meaning the inheritance and legacy—*and* the father's blessing, essential even if received through deception.*

Esau may be a little slow on the uptake, but eventually he figures out, or somebody explains to him, that he has been duped. He wants to go hunting again, but this time for a different quarry. Little Brother Season begins.

Jacob realizes he has scammed *himself*: he can't enjoy the prize he's won. That would require a fight, and Jacob doesn't do fights. He runs away.

After a long journey, Jacob connects with his uncle Laban and gets a steady job. He also falls in love with Laban's lovely daughter Rachel. The deal is for Jacob to work seven years

* This was before lawyers. Tough break.

to earn her hand in marriage. Those seven years pass—they actually go by quickly, we're told, because Jacob is in love. But then he finds out he's not the only con man on the ranch. Laban switches daughters on him on the wedding night.

Jacob wakes up the morning after and finds not Rachel but Rachel's sister Leah beside him. A furious Jacob confronts Laban, who talks him down and offers a new deal: seven more years and this time he gets Rachel, Scout's honor, no switcheroos.

We notice that over the years, Jacob is passive-aggressive in how he deals with Laban. He begins building wealth by accumulating his own livestock and embezzling the best of Laban's livestock. Lots of conning, conniving, grabbing, and deceiving go back and forth. Nobody wants to play Monopoly with this family.

Laban catches on to the cattle-rustling, and his anger forces Jacob to run away once again, this time with his family, servants, and possessions. Jacob gets a three-day head start on his pursuers, but eventually Laban catches up, and there's a confrontation. Jacob says, "I rushed away because I was afraid" (Gen. 31:31 NLT).

Up to this point, that verse is the story of Jacob's life. He manipulates, he's found out, he runs away because he's afraid. Instead of doing the hard thing, he turns and runs. What is that if not giving up?

I wonder how many of us show that pattern in our lives. It may not involve cattle or marriage fraud, but we have our own cycles of fear and flight. Our poor dealings catch up with us, and we take off again. Job to job. Relationship to relationship. Commitment to commitment. It becomes a vicious cycle that only grows worse.

If this is you, perhaps the weather is calm right now. You're still trying to control, still trying to fix things. This time it's going to work. You're sure you can outmaneuver whoever or whatever is coming after you. Outplay, outthink, and if all else fails, outrun.

We want to give up and run away from the mess that we've made.

She's afraid of picking the wrong degree and failing at career planning, so she withdraws from school. He feels bad about the financial situation they're in, but instead of talking to his wife about it, he buys more and more, hoping to keep distracting. She gossips about her coworker, but when her comments get back to him, she cuts him off instead of owning her failure and asking for forgiveness.

Maybe you've realized that, for all of your efforts to fix things, you've only made things worse. So you've withdrawn, at least emotionally. I mean, what's the point of even trying?

This is the fear of failure that I referenced earlier. When we find ourselves in a situation where we don't think we have what it takes, we run away. The problem is that fear distorts our perception of reality. It tells us late at night that the jacket strewn over the chair is some kind of monster or intruder.

Fear convinces us to give up before we've even tried.

Here are a few fears that I've noticed holding me back sometimes:

1. There's a difficult conversation I need to have with someone. I'm afraid of how he will respond, so I put it off. I know God wants me to do it, but I haven't done it yet.

2. I'm afraid of failing as a husband and a father. These things mean so much to me, but because they mean so much, I find myself operating out of fear. What if I fail? What if I'm not strong enough? What if I'm not wise enough? Those fears can sometimes make me run to work where it feels safer.

3. I'm afraid right now. I find myself running away from writing. What if I write this book and it doesn't connect with people? What if someone reviews it and takes something out of context? What if it just isn't very good?

This is what giving up may look like:

Running away before the race has even started.
Running from friendship to friendship.
Running from conflict to conflict.
Running from broken promise to broken promise.

There is no responsibility. No courage, no fighting through the night or getting to the blessing that comes in the morning.

Often in life, you'll find that if you just risk turning on the light, that fearsome monster is stripped of all power and is exposed for what it is: just a jacket draped over a chair. How many of our paralyzing fears are harmless props or potentials that never even materialize?

The challenge is real; I get that. We've all been there. But to step into your role as God sees you, sometimes you must choose to say, "Enough!" And maybe right now you can't say it from some grandiose, broad-shouldered Superman pose, but it's a gentle yet declarative faith-filled whisper to yourself: *Enough. I'm not running anymore.*

Fear causes most of us to run away. That's what Jacob did. That was his pattern, until finally there was nowhere to run. That's one potential that always becomes real: the place where there's nowhere else to run.

But before you give up and run away, you need to see what happens to Jacob.

Nowhere Left to Run

With no trust between them, Jacob and Laban can only settle their dispute through a borderline. Jacob cannot cross it. He agrees he will never set foot over that boundary, back onto Laban's land, again. Laban leaves and Jacob continues west toward his homeland. The problem is, Jacob's homeland is also Esau's. And Esau may still be hunting.

Laban on one side, Esau on the other, Jacob finds himself with nowhere left to run. Jacob hasn't seen Esau since cheating him out of his birthright and running away. So he sends a delegation with gifts and a message that he's coming in peace. Those men return with news—and it's ominous. They've met Esau, and he's heading their way with four hundred men (Gen. 32:6).

We read that Jacob is terrified. Who wouldn't be? For once, the opposite direction—his favorite place to flee—is cut off. He divides up his wives, his children, his servants, his livestock, and all of his possessions, so that when Esau attacks one group the other group will have time to escape. In other words, instead of fighting, he's diversifying, in hopes of minimizing his losses. He sends these two groups ahead.

Jacob stays behind by himself, presumably to see which group Esau confronts so he can then join the safe group. His family is in danger. His livelihood is threatened. And now, as a man of wealth, he has so much more to lose. Life has never seemed so deep down dark.

Genesis 32 tells of the amazing events that follow. Jacob finds himself all alone in a desolate clearing. Getting everyone sent off had been loud and chaotic. Now he sits in silence. He suddenly hears something behind him. The sound of footsteps getting closer. His first instinct is to run. But there is nowhere left to run. And it's too dark to see where he's going. I'm sure Jacob calls out for the person to identify himself. Jacob's heart is pounding in his chest. He can feel his adrenaline surging through his veins. The stranger grabs hold of Jacob and throws him to the ground. The two men begin to wrestle. They fight through the night, and as the sun begins to rise the man realizes that Jacob isn't going to quit. Not this time. The man reaches out and touches Jacob's hip, which then wrenches out of its socket, and cries out, "Let me go, for it is daybreak!"

Jacob says, "I will not let you go unless you bless me." Jacob realizes he has been wrestling with a supernatural messenger from God. Jacob knows how desperate his situation is; he realizes that his family is in danger and that his life hangs in the balance, so in his desperation he boldly insists on a blessing. Instead of giving up, Jacob asks God for help. He pleads for God's blessing. He won't stop until he gets it.

The stranger says, "Your name will no longer be Jacob, but Israel, because you have struggled with God and with humans and have overcome" (Gen. 32:28).

Jacob has a new name, but he wants to know the stranger's name. The challenger asks him why, then blesses him. And that's it. The sun rises and the "man" is gone.

We understand who this mysterious wrestler is. Jacob has been wrestling with God. He faced the fight he has avoided all his life. Like Jonah, like so many others in the Scriptures and in our lives, his lesson is that you can't run away from God.

But something has changed in Jacob. Once it's on, once he's wrestling, he won't stop until he gets a blessing out of it. This is the moment he goes from being Gypping Jacob to Chosen Israel. This is where the scheming, the fear, and the flight come to an end and the blessings begin.

Every good thing is possible. But not without a fight.

Gerald Sittser, a professor at Whitworth College in Spokane, Washington, was with some members of his family when the minivan they were traveling in was hit by a drunk driver. In that accident, he lost three generations. He lost his mom. He lost his wife. He lost his young daughter.

Gerald was somehow able to walk away uninjured, but it seemed like anything but a blessing. He wrote a book about what he went through entitled *A Grace Disguised*. Reflecting on a line from the poet Robert Frost, he tells us the path to blessing is not around but *through*. He puts it this way: "The quickest way for anyone to reach the sun and the light of day is not to run west, chasing after the setting sun, but to head east plunging into the darkness until one comes to the sunrise."[3]

Instead of running west, just plunge into the darkness. That's counterintuitive. If you even think about it, all your instincts rebel. We avoid desperation, simply hoping the situation clears itself up, waiting for the darkness to lighten. But what if the desperation is a grace disguised? What if fighting your way through the darkness is the path to blessing? The quickest way through the desperation may well be to embrace it. Plunge into it. Fight your way through the darkness.

Blessed and Broken

Jacob stops running and fights through the night. He doesn't give up, he doesn't flee, and a wrestling match changes everything.

First, he is blessed. The blessing comes when he is given a new name.

In verse 27, God asks Jacob, "What is your name?"

Obviously God knows the answer to that one. He's not drawing a blank—he's God.* Yet Jacob doesn't answer the question. Why?

I think I know. I think he's ashamed of his name. He knows what it means: *cheater, scoundrel, manipulator, conniver*. At that time in history, a name was especially significant. It was more than what people called you. A name was who you were. It was your identity. My guess is that Jacob had never liked his name because it labeled him. It revealed his character. "Hey, Conniver. Come here!"

His life has reinforced that label, so that to hear his name was to be told his sins. But in verse 28, God changes that name to something beautiful: *Israel*. "God strives."

This name is exclusively his. It isn't from his father. It isn't from his older brother, his uncle, or even from Abraham.

---

* You'll never hear God calling people buddy, pal, bro, or dude because he can't remember a name.

He's had to fight for this name. But it is his name, his achievement, his future, and his blessing. Something between God, one man, and nobody else.

So, here's a question. What exactly did Jacob do to earn this blessing? I would say his big accomplishment that night was not giving up. He kept fighting.

How did he fight? He hung on to God and refused to let go.

There is a lady who sits in the front row at the church where I preach. She and her husband, David, have sat in those seats every weekend for years. David and Annie always seem to engage with the message as they reference the open Bible that they share. David is a professional motivational speaker, so I know it would be easy for him to sit and criticize my delivery. But this couple is always positive and encouraging.

My eyes filled with tears when I learned that Annie had been diagnosed with breast cancer. I prayed for them and asked God to heal her and to fill her life with his courage. The cancer metastasized to her lymph nodes. She went from being a personal trainer to receiving radiation treatments five days a week. When she felt like giving up, she kept fighting. She wrestled. She hung on to God and refused to let go.

In the wrestling, she discovered a blessing. Here's the way she expressed it: "God took my physical brokenness and turned it into something wonderful. He did not make me like I was before cancer."

She talks about some of the gifts that God gave her in the struggle. She discovered a deeper joy. She developed greater mercy and love for others. She felt free from many of her fears and anxieties, because she had no other option but either to quit or to trust God. She found a new purpose and ministry for her life.

God doesn't want to leave you like you were before the addiction, or abuse, or affair, or relationship, or financial devastation, or diagnosis, or failure. He wants to bless you and introduce you to a whole new world of meaning and opportunity. But sometimes you have to fight through the night to get to the blessing.

Jacob receives a blessing from God. He is given a new name. But he doesn't escape without a scar. Verse 25 records that during the course of this wrestling match, the man touches Jacob's hip. The Hebrew word translated "touch" literally means a light tap. It's like gently touching someone on the shoulder when you don't want to startle them.

Which gives you a clear indication that the angel of the Lord had dialed it down for this cage match—like an MMA champion who is wrestling with his toddler son. This "light tap" is enough to rip Jacob's hip out of its socket. Though Jacob is given a new name, he will walk with pain and a noticeable limp for the rest of his life.

When you don't give up, there is a blessing for you on the other side, but that doesn't mean you won't have a limp. Jacob wrestles with God and comes out of the match both blessed and broken. He has a limp that he's going to have to live with, but the limp is a reminder of the blessing. He has a scar now, but when he sees it, he remembers the struggle and the blessing that came from it.

Maybe you can look back at a time in your life when you were ready to call it quits, but instead of giving up, you turned to God and fought through it. In hindsight, you wouldn't ever want to go through that again, but you're thankful that you did. My wife's grandfather was a pilot in World War II. When he talks about being in battle, he describes it this way: "I wouldn't give you a nickel to go through that again, but I wouldn't trade it for a million dollars."

It was hard. It was painful. It's still difficult to talk about. But he's thankful for what he learned and the man it made him on the other side: blessed and broken.

Jacob is reunited with his family and servants, and eventually he has no other option than to come face-to-face with Esau—his older, stronger, warrior brother whom he has cheated out of an inheritance. Jacob prepares a generous gift, hoping it will appease Esau's anger. When Esau is still a ways off, Jacob bows down to his brother. And he looks up to see his older brother running right at him. Taking him in his arms. Pulling him tight, kissing him with tears of joy.

The two of them stand there, arms wrapped around each other's necks, crying without shame (Gen. 33:4).

It's a beautiful scene, and also a sad one—sad because it took so much longer than necessary. Whole decades of brotherly camaraderie have been lost. Maybe Esau wasn't ready until then. But maybe he was. Maybe a month after it happened, his heart started to soften. Maybe it was a year after the betrayal when the bitterness finally melted away. If Jacob had summoned the courage to humble himself sooner, maybe this family would have been reunited twenty years earlier.

If you have the courage to stop running and decide that you are going to fight through the darkness and not give up until you reach the other side, you will discover God's power and presence. But you may also discover a reconciled relationship, a renewed purpose, or a new identity and hope for the future.

Don't Let Go

Across the world and thousands of years after Jacob, thousands of feet underground in a Chilean mine, revival was breaking out. Thirty-three miners sat in utter darkness yet with their souls bathed in new light. They were crying out to God and feeling his grace. Up top, a rescue operation was proceeding furiously. Maybe you saw the news coverage. An elite drill team gathered and the Chilean miners were rescued.

If you find yourself in the deep down dark, I know that instinctively you'll just want to get out of there. You'll want the night to come to an end. I get it. But when you most feel like giving up, you are best positioned to experience God's presence. It's a strange thing that God can often be seen most clearly in the darkness of life. The quiet allows you to hear him speak. The isolation allows you to connect with him. You'll never encounter a better time to discover what he's all about.

So, here's an idea. Instead of running away from the darkness, run into it. Instead of tapping out, grab hold of God and don't let go. He has a blessing for you, but you may need to fight for it.

The deep down dark may be a hospital waiting room. It may be the inside of a courtroom. It may be a funeral home or a juvenile detention center. Maybe it's a motel room, because your wife has told you you're no longer welcome in your own home.

Some of you are reading these words in a prison cell. You feel hurt. You feel overwhelmed. You feel helpless. You feel lonely. You feel scared. More than anything, you want to get out. You would pay almost any price, accept almost any deal that offered you escape.

I understand. But instead of running, maybe it's time to fight. If you'll grab hold of God and refuse to let go, you'll find that there is a gift for you there. He will give you himself.

In your loneliness, there is an opportunity to discover his presence.

In your fear, there is an opportunity to discover his peace.

In your weakness, there is an opportunity to discover his strength.

In your pain, there is an opportunity to discover his purpose.

In your shame, there is an opportunity to discover his grace.

In your darkness, there is an opportunity to discover his light.

Jacob would've had a story to tell about his limp. Every wound, every scar has a story to tell. The scar on my leg is from a bike accident, when Andy Ward jumped on unexpectedly. The scar on my arm is from Terry Good dropping a board with a rusty nail on me while we were building a fort.

If you know someone with an obvious scar, or you have a buddy with a bad knee or a bum shoulder, ask them what happened, and you'll be rewarded with a story. The story Jacob told had to be a doozy.

"Hey, Jacob—why do you walk so funny?"

"Well, first of all it's not Jacob—it's Israel. And I'll tell you how it happened. I got in a wrestling match with God, and we fought all night. I refused to give up until he blessed me."

I bet Jacob told that story at every family gathering, every class reunion, and every office party. No matter what story someone else told around the table, Jacob always had one to beat it. "Kids, have I ever told you about the time I wrestled with God? It was late at night, and the woods were silent . . ."

Maybe his grandchildren rolled their eyes. Maybe they'd heard it one too many times. "Here we go again—the wrestling story . . ."

Whether they admitted it or not, however, I bet they loved hearing those familiar words. Because if they lived long enough, they likely found it was their story too. It can be everybody's story. It's a redemption story. A story of darkness giving way to dawn, of curse giving way to blessing, of a wound that actually heals a life.

If you've run until you're exhausted, if you feel cornered and afraid, if you have nowhere else to turn and the darkness has become complete—Jacob has a story for you. And it ends this way: "Stop running. Don't take another step, because you're running away from a blessing. Take hold of it now. Fight for it. And never, never give up."

3

Keep Perspective

Did you ever hear the story of American swimmer Florence Chadwick? She became the first woman to swim the English Channel both ways. She also attempted to swim from Catalina Island to the coastline of California.

What made her failed attempt so newsworthy was the reason she didn't make it. It wasn't the cold water or muscle cramps. It wasn't sharks or a school of jellyfish. It wasn't even the physical exhaustion of a sixteen-hour swim. The reason she quit was fog.

When the fog rolled in, she wasn't able to see the coastline and had to quit. When she climbed into the boat, she was informed that she was less than one mile from the shore. If only she'd known how close she was, she could have persevered. Instead, she lost perspective and gave up.

There are times in life when the fog rolls in and we lose sight of the shore. Someone you trusted takes advantage of you. Someone you love stops loving you in return. A good plan goes off the rails. Unexpected physical or financial hardships come fast and hard. When the fog is thick, it's easy to lose perspective. We think things are worse than they are. Without realizing it, we start to feel sorry for ourselves. We quit and then we blame the fog so we won't feel like a quitter. It's not that we wanted to give up; it's just our unfair circumstances made it impossible to keep going.

I didn't want to give up my marriage, but after what my spouse did to me, I didn't have a choice. I didn't want to give up on my dream to start a new business, but the economy is killing me.

I didn't want to give up on church, but the new pastor can't even remember my name. I didn't want to give up on our commitment to be generous, but we've had to deal with so many unexpected health challenges.

In the midst of difficult situations and painful circumstances, we often lose faith because we lose perspective. All we can see is our immediate hurt. It seems immense at the time. Yet a little perspective can change everything.

Two months after her first try, Florence Chadwick made another attempt. Again the fog was quite heavy. Again she couldn't see the coastline—but this time she finished the swim. She said that this time, when the fog rolled in, she kept a mental image of the shoreline in her mind and focused on that. She kept perspective and refused to give up.

Hebrews 12:1 reminds us that "we are surrounded by such a great cloud of witnesses." You may remember that a witness is someone who says something. Many of these witnesses are named, like Abraham and Jacob. We're invited to carry their stories in our hearts when we're weary. We feel their encouragement: "The coastline is so close! Keep swimming!"

Those two and others are the "celebrity" faith heroes, big-name Bible people beloved by everybody. But there are also witnesses whose names aren't given. Did they accomplish less? You be the judge:

> There were others who were tortured, refusing to be released so that they might gain an even better resurrection. Some faced jeers and flogging, and even chains and imprisonment. They were put to death by stoning; they were sawed in two; they were killed by the sword. They went about in sheepskins and goatskins, destitute, persecuted and mistreated—the world was not worthy of them. They wandered in deserts and mountains, living in caves and in holes in the ground. (Heb. 11:35–38)

They carried out lives of obscure greatness. One message these unnamed witnesses might have for us is to keep perspective the next time we're struggling with discouragement.

The next time you feel like your situation isn't fair and you're ready to give up, remember those who faced jeers and flogging, chains and imprisonment. Consider these heroes of the faith who were put to death by stoning and being sawed in two—and are not even mentioned by name in Scripture.

If they could find the faith to keep believing and keep going, then you can make it through what you're going through—not to diminish in any way what you're going through. You may be dealing with a devastating loss, debilitating pain, or unbearable trauma. You may be enduring suffering that I couldn't begin to imagine. I'm not questioning the pain that you feel, but I do want you to keep perspective. You're not the only one to have felt what you're feeling. There are others, like the unnamed witnesses in Hebrews 11, who have endured and persevered in the face of incredible suffering.

I think they would say to you, "I'm so sorry for what you're going through. The pain and injustice of this world can feel overwhelming. But don't give up. Take it a day at a time. God will give you enough strength for today. His grace is sufficient."

There are many of us, however, who might need a more challenging message. In the cloud of witnesses, they'll come right out and say what needs to be said—at least, that's the way I imagine them. It's tough for me to visualize any of them offering platitudes or a pat on the back. The tough love tool is right where they can grab it on short notice as the need arises. To some of us, they might say, "Stop feeling sorry for yourself."

Yes, I know. It seems a little harsh. *Life* is harsh. Pain is painful. Hurting *hurts*—and now this book wants to pile on?

Trials are trying, but they don't last forever. Don't spend your life feeling sorry for yourself. As long as you decide to see yourself as a victim, you won't experience the taste of victory.

Victim Mentality

One of the ways you know it may be time to stop feeling sorry for yourself is that you feel defensive when some meddling-book pipes up and tells you to stop feeling sorry for yourself.

When people tell you to stop feeling sorry for yourself, it's hurtful. And you start feeling sorry for yourself. If this sounds like you, stay with me.

People who pity themselves and live with a victim mentality rarely realize it. That's especially true when the people around them are constantly reinforcing it. Well-meaning friends and family often reinforce a victim mentality because they see our pain and try to comfort us with the nearest tools in their emotional toolshed: sympathy and pity. That tough love tool is always in the very back of the shed, where it's nearly impossible to get to.

A victim mentality can be hard to self-diagnose because it's not always pervasive. You may not be one to throw an all-encompassing pity party, but it's just possible you're struggling with a stubborn little pocket of victim mentality. Perhaps there's a specific area of your life you assume can never change. In that area, instead of taking personal responsibility, you blame others. What is it? Your marriage? Career? Parenting? Financial situation? An addiction? Inability to maintain a healthy relationship?

One way to identify an area where you have a victim mentality is to pinpoint an area of your life where you're tempted to give up.

It's so hard to see in ourselves. For that reason, I thought I'd offer a special mirror to help you discern if this might be you. So take a look at the following features and consider whether you may be feeling sorry for yourself, or at least have a victim mentality in some area of your life.

People with a victim mentality tend to whine and complain.

They feel powerless to change, so they lament their circumstances. They focus on what's wrong and ignore what's right. They can offer exhaustive lists of the ways they've been treated unfairly and gotten the short end of the stick.

Journalist James Glassman declares that a "culture of complaint" has infected America. For instance, we complain about low incomes, high food prices, and the outsourcing of jobs. However:

- Adjusting for inflation, compensation has tripled since 1947, while the cost of necessities has plummeted.
- Food in 1950 represented about one-third of a family's total expenditures; today, it's one-seventh.
- Americans work fewer hours and have more cars, cultural institutions, and children in college than ever before.[1]

Turns out at least some of our complaining isn't justified. I have a feeling a lot of the rest of it isn't either.

A whiny, complaining spirit is a dangerous quality because it leads to quitting. You can tell when someone is close to quitting a job because they constantly complain. Think about going on what promises to be a long hike with someone who starts whining and complaining during the first mile. *It's too hot. I'm getting hungry. These shoes aren't very comfortable. My knee is starting to hurt. I'm getting eaten up by mosquitoes.*

It's not going to be long before you hear, *I'm done. Let's go back.*

People with a victim mentality tend to blame and criticize.

The cardinal quality of someone who feels sorry for themselves is a refusal to take responsibility. Some people give up by blaming God. They say things like,

God did this to me by allowing this to happen.
God hasn't answered my prayers.

God could heal me, but he hasn't.
God should have protected me.

Some blame others. They might say,

If my parents hadn't been so strict . . .
If my husband were more attentive . . .
If my wife were more affectionate . . .
If my boss just acknowledged how talented I am . . .

On the rare occasion I do marriage counseling, I've found that a couple often wants to spend the majority of the session telling on each other. He wants to tell me how he's the victim; she wants to tell me why I should feel sorry for her. Their marriage is in trouble, and they're both ready to give up, but instead of taking responsibility, they blame each other. The fog moves in.

Yet the shore is so close! If they would only keep perspective and push forward instead of against the current.

People with a victim mentality tend to be cynical and pessimistic.

Try telling them things are going to get better if they don't give up. They'll look at you as if you've said the sky is green, and they'll assure you you're wrong—any fool knows it never gets better, because:

I've been exercising, but the scale says the same thing.
I've gone out on a couple of dates, but I know it won't
    work out.

I've worked really hard, but my boss is never going to give me a raise.

Pessimism is the next block down from self-pity. And self-pity is the last stop before giving up.

Change Your Perspective

I know that for me, choosing not to feel sorry for myself comes much easier when I get a little dose of true perspective. If I'm having a difficult season in ministry, I might start feeling sorry for myself—and then I spend some time with my friend Edry, who is a Haitian pastor.

Edry lives in a two-bedroom shack with his wife and children. No windows. Electricity that rarely works. He spends his days preaching the gospel up in the hills, while his wife works at the market to earn a consistent income. All I need to do is think about Edry and his joyful spirit, and suddenly my situation doesn't seem so bad.

Or maybe something in life reminds me that a missionary we support has been stoned for preaching the gospel. Really. That still happens, you know. He survived, but people actually responded to his preaching by throwing stones at him. So when I talk to him, I don't complain. I don't say, "You wouldn't believe the nasty email I got from someone in the church. I'm so discouraged."*

What's he going to say to that? "You mean you had a mean person send you harsh electronic correspondence? How must that feel?"

* Also I don't mention that sometimes no one brings fried chicken to the potluck after church. Or they bring "original" instead of "extra crispy."

He's not going to feel sorry for me, which is a pretty good cue for me to stop feeling sorry for myself.

Sometimes I get my minimum daily requirement of perspective by reading accounts of heroes of the faith who aren't even mentioned in Hebrews 11, even anonymously. Yes, Hebrews 11 isn't exhaustive when it comes to faith heroes— Christian history is pretty well loaded down with them.

For example, Adoniram Judson was a missionary to Burma, where he established sixty-three churches and personally led over six thousand Burmese to faith in Christ. But it wasn't easy. He was twenty-two when he made the decision to leave America to become a missionary. He set sail for India. But when he and his pregnant wife arrived, they wouldn't let him in.

For three weeks, the two of them were stuck at sea. His wife gave birth on that boat in the middle of the storm, and the baby died. They did get to shore, and for the first six and a half years, he shared the gospel every day. Not one person in Burma came to faith. Financial supporters in America backed away and told him it was time to come home. He was scattering the seeds faithfully, even sacrificially, yet God would bring no harvest.

He kept perspective. Kept praying. Kept preaching. Judson was eventually put in prison for that preaching. He would be chained so that his back, shoulders, and head were on the ground and his legs would be held high off the ground in stocks. For a period of several years, he was in that position. He slept, ate, and used the restroom in that position.

His wife and three children would die in Burma. His second wife and their two children would also die in Burma. Time and time again, he could have felt sorry for himself and quit, but he never gave up.

It was anything but easy. And he could have decided to quit. There were any number of easy careers back home. But he loved Jesus and was certain in his calling. So he chose to persevere. Today there are some 3,700 churches in Burma that trace their beginning to the day Adoniram Judson set sail from America.

When I told Judson's story in church, three young men came up to me after the service and introduced themselves. They explained to me that they were visiting the United States from Burma. They had all become Christians at a Burmese church. Its name was Judson Church. It turns out some of those seeds brought a harvest after all.

When I intentionally look at my situation and challenges from the perspective of Judson—or countless others—I can actually *try* to feel sorry for myself, but I can't do it. Instead, I'm inspired and filled with courage to keep going and not give up.

Sometimes when I need a little perspective I simply look out into the congregation of the church where I preach. I can usually spot Jenny Smith sitting in her wheelchair with a smile on her face. I asked her if she would share some of her story with you.

As a sixteen-year-old, I never had a vision of what I wanted my future to be like. I loved gymnastics, playing piano, and coaching. But I wasn't sure where that would take me.

Then, on July 11, 1989, I sustained a C6-7 spinal cord injury and became a quadriplegic.

That morning, I slipped on dew-covered grass while tumbling. I was an accomplished gymnast, but this time the wet grass caused an injury that changed my life; I lost the use of my hands and legs in a split second.

So much changed in that moment. I was no longer able to do gymnastics, play keyboard for a band, play piano in church, participate in cheerleading at school, or play varsity volleyball. My identity was lost, along with everything I loved doing.

I refocused on doing what I could from my wheelchair. I made school a priority, graduating early from high school, then went on to get a master's degree in counseling psychology.

Did I ever lose hope? Not entirely. Partly, I think, because hope was all I had left. I clung to the belief that God could continue to use me. Hebrews 6:19 says, "We have this hope as an anchor for the soul, firm and secure." Hope is what kept me living. Not just living, but living abundantly (John 10:10).

Not giving up required me to find the courage to say yes to things outside my comfort zone. I traveled to Mexico to distribute wheelchairs. In time I became the vice president of the organization taking wheelchairs around the world. I loved working with others who have disabilities in Mexico, Costa Rica, El Salvador, and the place my heart aches for: Afghanistan. For the last nine years, I've been working with a mission organization supporting cross-cultural workers as they live overseas.

Through playing wheelchair tennis, rugby, and rowing on the Ohio River, I learned how to become more independent in my daily life. I bought my own condo and live by myself.

While I am thankful for all that God has done, I would be lying if I told you that I haven't felt discouraged, frustrated, and even humiliated at the dependency created by a spinal cord injury. But it has required me to lean on God in a way that I might not have done otherwise.

It has challenged me to reach out to others and ask for prayer for renewed hope. And God has always been faithful. He wants the same for you—just say yes to what he has. Don't give up hope.

Talk to Yourself

The Bible repeatedly puts emphasis on our thought lives. We are transformed by the renewing of our minds. We take every thought captive, because we understand that every little thought has tremendous power over us. Paul, who knew something about suffering and the need for perspective, writes, "Whatever is true, whatever is noble, whatever is right, whatever is pure, whatever is lovely, whatever is admirable—if anything is excellent or praiseworthy—think about such things" (Phil. 4:8).

One way we control our thought life is through self-talk. We all talk to ourselves. We are, each of us, our own all-day, all-talk radio stations with one devoted listener. Are the programs encouraging or discouraging? Our thoughts have incredible power in our lives, and if our self-talk is self-defeating, we'll feel like quitting.

On the other hand, encouraging self-talk can be life-giving. We see this in the psalms. For example, here is David allowing us to listen in on his inner monologue:

> Why, my soul, are you downcast?
>   Why so disturbed within me?
> Put your hope in God,
>   for I will yet praise him,
>   my Savior and my God. (Ps. 42:5)

My sports psychologist friend told me about the power of a mantra. A mantra is a personal motto or maxim that we strategically tell ourselves repeatedly. More than just one-time encouraging self-talk, these words of David seem to be a personal mantra. We see him speak them to himself in verse 5, again in verse 11, then again in Psalm 43:5.

Why does he keep saying the same thing to himself? We know a good bit about David's life. He had good reason to feel tempted to be downcast and discouraged. But he refused to throw a pity party; instead, he used self-talk strategically to encourage himself and to keep himself from quitting.

Self-talk is speaking courage into yourself.

We choose our thoughts in the same way we choose a TV show or what to eat for dinner. At any time, we can change the channel or the menu. When self-pity begins to come on, it's time to see what else is playing.

Trading Pity for Praise

One of the most effective ways to keep perspective and stop responding with self-pity is to realize how much we have to be thankful for. We see this in the life of Paul. Even when he is unjustly imprisoned, he writes in his prison cell, "Rejoice in the Lord always. I will say it again: Rejoice!" (Phil. 4:4).

When you're most inclined to respond with self-pity, ask God to show you what you have to be thankful for. Scrape away every trace of self-pity and replace it with a fresh coat of praise.

I'm on a flight to Orlando, Florida. I'm sitting behind a mom and her son, who is probably seven or eight. She's in the aisle seat, he's in the center seat, and some poor, random soul is sitting by the window. I don't need to be paying much attention to conclude that the mom and the boy are en route to Disney World. He's rocking a bright Mickey Mouse shirt, and his mother is telling him about all the wonderful rides and attractions. But he isn't paying attention to that; he's throwing a fit because he doesn't have the window seat.

You're on your way to the Magic Kingdom, but life's not fair because you don't have a window seat. Sound familiar?

Now I'm at the ballpark for Little League. A father is sitting in the bleachers, overheating, blowing a gasket because his son struck out. He yells at his son, who is walking sadly to the dugout, "What's wrong with you? Keep your eye on the ball!"

Then he turns his attention to the umpire and starts in on *him*. Other parents stare awkwardly at their hands.

Bro—it's a beautiful day. Your son is healthy and strong. You are one of the 8 percent of the global population who own a car to bring you here. You have enough free time to watch your boy play.

I have an idea: stop feeling sorry for yourself and start finding reasons to be thankful.

I read a testimony recently of a woman who returned from a mission trip. She had gone to the island of Tobago, where she worked with a leper colony. On the last day of her trip, she was leading worship for the colony when she asked if anyone had a favorite song. She saw a woman toward the back raise her hand. The woman's face was completely disfigured. She had no ears and no nose; her lips were gone.

But she smiled, raised a fingerless hand, and asked, "Could we sing the hymn 'Count Your Blessings,' please?"

What You Don't Know

When you look at your circumstances and start to lose perspective, it helps to underline a basic plot point: you don't really know what God is up to in your life.

You have no idea how he might use what you're going through. Knowing his past work, my best guess is that it will be impressive and seem to come out of nowhere, if you ever find out what it was.

Did you see the news story about Mary Ann Franco? Mary Ann lost her eyesight in 1995 and spent decades in darkness. In August 2015, she took a hard fall and injured her neck. She spent the next ten months in pain and discouragement. Her life as a blind person was challenging enough, but now she had chronic pain.

Mary Ann said she had always maintained her faith in God, but I imagine she must have questioned why he would allow such things. Eventually she had an operation to alleviate the pain in her arm and back. When she came out of surgery—*she could see*. The surgery had somehow restored her sight. The neurosurgeon was asked for an explanation and he came up empty. There absolutely wasn't one. Why should he have known what God was up to? Nobody else did.

Faith gives us a confidence in what we cannot see so that we can accept that life is difficult. That kind of faith gives us a perspective on our current struggles. We don't feel sorry for ourselves now because we have confidence in what awaits. Faith understands that our best life isn't now; our best life is yet to come. So we don't grow weary or lose heart.

Choose to Overcome

Not only will we choose not to feel sorry for ourselves because of our circumstances but we will also choose to overcome our circumstances.

Instead of feeling like a victim, we choose to use what's happened to us as a springboard propelling us to greatness.

Sound overly optimistic? A little too Tony Robbins for you?

It's not. This is the power of God in your life. Paul reminds us in Ephesians 1:19–20 that the same power that brought Jesus back from the dead is available to us. The power that overcame death can help us overcome our circumstances. Our confidence to overcome is not a confidence in ourselves but in the power of the Holy Spirit, who is in us.

The truth is, life is difficult for everyone. Some choose to be defeated. Others choose to overcome. Interestingly, it's often the people who have faced the most difficulty who succeed the most wildly.

For instance, did you know that two-thirds of British prime ministers, at the peak of their empire, and almost a third of all US presidents lost a parent when they were children? And did you know that about a third of successful entrepreneurs are dyslexic? That could all be some wild coincidence, but I don't think so. What would happen if you began to view your struggles as a springboard to something incredible?

In his book *David and Goliath*, Malcolm Gladwell shares those statistics, along with stories of multitudes of people who chose to overcome. He writes about what he calls "desirable difficulties," postulating that having to face horrible circumstances is actually an opportunity rather than an obstacle.[2] People who have to overcome adversity are forced to learn more and work harder, and actually have an advantage over those who have had it easier. The few, the chosen—the strugglers.

He suggests that the unbelievable number of people who have overcome disability or disadvantage didn't succeed in *spite* of their circumstances but *because* of them. Not that difficulties served up greatness to them on a silver platter. Instead, they chose to use their difficulties as fuel for the journey.

All of these people chose to overcome, and you can too. In fact, you have something going for you that many of them didn't: *God.* Romans 8:37 reads, "We are more than conquerors through him who loved us." Speak those words to your soul the next time the fog rolls in and you feel like giving up.

Life is difficult, but nothing you've faced or are facing is too difficult for him. His grace is sufficient for you, and his power is made perfect in your weakness (2 Cor. 12:9). So, if you've felt like quitting, I'm telling you: listen to what the great cloud of witnesses is saying to you.

In the cloud of witnesses there is a group of big names and also a group of people whose names we don't know. They wore sheepskins and goatskins, wandered in deserts, and hid in caves. The world, we're told, was not worthy of them. I wonder what they would say if they looked at your current situation. Maybe it would be something like, "Would you stop it, please? For your own sake and for the sake of people around you, would you stop feeling sorry for yourself?

"Look, I know that what happened to you wasn't right. I know what happened to you wasn't fair. I get that what you're going through hurts, and it hurts a lot.

"Life is difficult. But what happened, happened. What you're going through is what you're going through. This is not the time to throw up your hands and quit. You may not see it right now. You may not understand it right now. You may be ready to turn back right now, just before you reach the far coastline.

"Don't. Just don't.

"Keep perspective, have faith, and don't give up."

SECTION 2

Throw Off the Weight

Sometimes we think we need comfort when what we really need is courage. This is what we've learned so far.

Sometimes what we want is sympathy when what we're really missing is strength.

Sometimes we want someone to feel sorry for us when what we really need is someone to challenge us.

When we grow tired and worn out, we may want the coach to tell us to get a drink and come take a breather on the bench. Our true need is for a coach to say, "Suck it up. Get in the game and finish this thing. You've got this!"

In Hebrews 12, the author is challenging believers not to give up. He first reminds the reader that we are surrounded by a great cloud of witnesses. The faith and faithfulness of our heroes gives us the confidence to keep believing and the courage to keep going.

When we grow weary, we remember those who have gone before us. The witnesses from that cloud speak to us and fill us with inspiration. They watch us, and we want to make them proud. It's the ultimate race: after running their leg of the relay, the sprinters come to the sidelines and cheer on the new carriers of the baton. Maybe you'll take your place in the cloud someday.

Here's the next thing the writer of Hebrews says to those who are growing weary and losing heart: "Let us throw off everything that hinders and the sin that so easily entangles" (Heb. 12:1).

Translation: cast off ballast.

The phrase translated as "throw off" comes from a compound word in the Greek. It could be translated "to lay something down and push it beyond reach." The writer speaks to those who are worn out and ready to give up. He tells them to identify what is weighing on them, set it down, and kick it away.

I was recently in a meeting. On the table, right in front of me, was a candy bowl. Candy bowls don't usually trip me up, because they tend to be filled with chocolate, and I don't really care for chocolate.* But this candy bowl had been filled with Starbursts, and Starbursts can definitely tangle me up. I've been known to accept Starbursts as currency. You can pay me in Starbursts or cash; I'm good with either.

As I sat in this meeting I picked up the candy bowl, set it on my lap, and ate three or four Starbursts without making a conscious decision to do so. Then I realized what I was doing. I set the bowl back on the table and told myself I wasn't going to eat anymore.

* I know some of you feel like you can no longer trust me.

Ten minutes later, I looked down to see that my hands were unwrapping yet another one. Who told my hands to do that? Something more drastic needed to be done. I grabbed the bowl, got up out of my chair, walked across the room, and set it on a table where I wouldn't be able to reach it.

I understand that Starbursts so easily entangle me. I wasn't just putting the bowl down—I was pushing it out of reach.

We identify what's tripping us up or slowing us down and we move it out of reach.

Look back at the words chosen: "Let us throw off." This isn't a mild suggestion. It's a direct charge to use your strength, whether physical, emotional, or volitional, depending on the situation, and throw the item away. Get up, grab hold of the bowl, and throw it to the other side of the room.

The author is calling your true, God-empowered self out from the slumber sin lulls us into. The message? "Wake up and deal with it!"

And yes, "throwing off" implies something is on you. You can only know that something's on you if you feel it, experience it, or see its effects. The challenge is to identify these things in your life that are weighing you down and take action so that you will not grow weary and lose heart.

Hebrews gives us two different categories to describe how our entanglements cause us to quit:

1. Everything that hinders
2. The sin that so easily entangles

The tendency is to read over this sentence quickly and to assume that these are one category. A cursory reading makes it sound like the author is defining what hinders *as* the sin that so easily entangles. That's one way to interpret it, but I would argue that he is moving from the general to the specific. The athlete avoids extra weight, but in training finds new ways to avoid the tiniest excess.

The Greeks, during the time when Hebrews was written, enjoyed their sporting events. They did think up the Olympics, after all. Greek runners trained with leg weights, then cast them aside when they were ready to run their race. As a matter of fact, they used extra weights in training for other sports too: hurdles and swimming, for examples. The weights built strength, but when they were cast away, the athlete was lighter, freer, stronger, and ready to excel— particularly as a runner. Greek runners also ran naked or almost naked, avoiding even the weight of clothing.

Thankfully, naked sprints haven't come back into style.* But runners today do avoid extra weight, down to special shoelaces. Every extra pound carried, according to one study, adds 1.4 seconds to a mile run.[1] Running shoes are rigorously tested to be as light as possible and still get the job done. Casual joggers don't worry about it. They carry their phones, maybe a bottle of water, a cap—dedicated runners throw off everything that slows them down.

Then, if they're talking serious racing, they get *specific*, cutting their hair, getting the lightest shoes and lightest clothing possible, because every ounce hinders. It so easily entangles.

That word *hinders* is actually a noun that means "any kind of weight." The New Living Translation puts Hebrews 12:1 this way: "Let us strip off every weight that slows us down."

---

* I think we can all agree that the .00002 seconds a pair of running shorts adds to a runner's time is acceptable.

In the next few chapters, we'll identify some of the common weights that hinder us. These weights aren't the same for everyone, but there's some dead weight that most of us struggle with. Carrying anything extra will slow you down, but if you carry it long enough, you will reach a point where you can't keep going. That's when you might give up.

This section is about what to lose and how to lose it.

4

Unhindered by Anxiety

Roller coaster stuck.

Try googling that phrase; you'll be surprised how often it turns up. Relatively speaking, it is not too often. But once is too many.

Just this week, I read about a roller coaster at an amusement park in Texas getting stuck. The ride clicked to the top, the riders prepared to be thrilled—and nothing happened. The cars halted on their tracks. Passengers peered over the edge with queasy stomachs. Any moment, they might just lurch downward at rocket speed. Or not. The hands that had been raised in the air now gripped the harness with white knuckles.

For forty-five minutes, they waited like that. On edge. Overwhelmed. Stressed out. Anxiety churning.

Anxiety is slowing down everyone. All you need to do is pay attention to what's happening around us, and you'll find that out. In his book *Anxiety Free*, psychologist Robert Leahy points out that "the average child today exhibits the same level of anxiety as the average psychiatric patient in the 1950s."[1]

Symptoms of anxiety are usually described as fear, nervousness, irritability, sleeplessness, and feeling overwhelmed. But wait, there's more: breathing difficulties, chest pain, concentration problems, digestive issues, headaches, insomnia, muscle tension, and low energy. Anxiety can even cause disturbing and obsessive thoughts, memory loss, and forgetfulness.

Anxiety can have a strong effect on your emotions. It can overwhelm and alter the serotonin and dopamine systems of the brain. It can surface in agitation, anger, and just a general sense of annoyance and make you feel moody, lonely, sad, and depressed. Anxiety can even cause body odor, hair loss, and excess armpit sweat.*

For some people, anxiety is more likely to take the form of physical symptoms. I have friends who would say they never feel anxious. They're not conscious of feeling stressed out or overwhelmed. But anxiety can steal in as the true source of aches, pains, and stiffness. It can cause blood pressure and circulation problems, hormone imbalance, hypertension, migraines, and weight gain or weight loss. Name pretty much anything bad, and anxiety can get it done.†

After presenting his research on the prevalence of anxiety, Dr. Leahy concluded, "We live in the Age of Anxiety. . . . We've become a nation of nervous wrecks."[2]

There are countless side effects to anxiety, but they add up to one significant outcome: giving up. As much as any weight we carry, the weight of anxiety can become so heavy

---

* Explains a lot of middle age men.
† Now you can feel anxious about being anxious. You're welcome.

that it feels impossible to keep going. It can be so crushing that taking even another step seems unbearable.

To one degree or another, anxiety is a weight we all carry. For some this weight is crushing, and for others it's merely annoying. On the anxiety spectrum, there are some of you who suffer from PTSD due to some trauma or abuse from your past, and you never feel safe. You're almost always in a fight, flight, or freeze response. You never know what might trigger it.

Some of you have a diagnosed anxiety disorder, and for you, anxiety is more than a spiritual issue. A friend of mine who helps people with anxiety says that sometimes we are praying for restored hearts, yet what a person needs is restored serotonin levels.

Others of you have trouble sleeping because you can't stop thinking about everything you need to get done. Or maybe your commute home from work is stressing you out. Maybe the holidays trigger your worry reflex; you feel overwhelmed. Family issues will do it too.

Wherever you are on the anxiety spectrum, I believe God wants to take away the weight you've been carrying. If you could learn to hand it over to him, it would change the way you run your race. Imagine feeling strong, loose, and free rather than straining under a burden.

It's not an easy thing. I get that the weight feels all too real, as it simultaneously pulls you down while pressing you into submission. It's legitimately heavy, and it begins with everyday thoughts—*What will my day be like?* And gradually the hows and what-ifs stage a takeover in your mind. What began as a simple tiptoeing around your thoughts in comfortable slippers has turned out to be heavy sprinting in ten-pound ankle weights. You're tired, worn, and just exhausted, and you feel like giving up.

As the new Christian community grew, followers of Christ felt stressed out and overwhelmed. Jesus's disciple Peter, once a fisherman and now a leader, wrote to encourage them as they faced the prospect of arrest and execution under the emperor Nero.

Peter begins his letter by addressing his readers as "God's elect, exiles scattered throughout" (1 Pet. 1:1). They've been driven out of their homes; many of them are living as refugees. They've lost their jobs. Their possessions have been seized, and they've been separated from friends and family.

That's a lot of weight they're trying to carry as they run the race. Their legs are tiring. They don't know how much farther they can go under this kind of stress.

Here's what Peter says to them: "Cast all your anxiety on him because he cares for you" (5:7).

Oh, okay. So that's it, then? Just cast it on him and it's all good? Hey, everybody, Peter figured it out! Yeah, if you feel overwhelmed by anxiety and fear, here's what you do: cast all your anxiety on God. Problem solved.

If you are overwhelmed by the weight you are carrying, a verse like this doesn't seem to help when someone lays it on you. It feels a bit naïve and maybe even a little offensive. Am I right? I think of the people I know who are struggling under the weight of their anxiety, and a verse like this comes off as a bit simplistic and ignorant.

I understand that. But let me ask you something: What if you really believed that last part—that the God of all creation cares about you?

Whether or not you see this verse as lame or powerful depends on what you believe about God. Do you believe he cares? That he can be trusted? My guess is that your willingness to believe a verse like this has a lot to do with what you're dealing with in life right now. Peter himself had some well-documented moments in life when he wasn't so sure.

In the fourth chapter of Mark, we read about Jesus putting his disciples in a boat and instructing them to go to the other side of the lake. Suddenly a huge storm comes upon them and waves start splashing into the boat. Remember, a number of the disciples are fishermen; they've weathered a few storms. But this one is something else. The Bible assures us they're terrified.

In the middle of the storm, one of them notices that Jesus is sleeping on a cushion in the stern of the ship. Just taking a nap. Panicked, Peter and the disciples start shaking Jesus—*Wake up! Wake up!*

Here's the question they have for him: "Don't you care if we drown?" (Mark 4:38).

For some of you, that's exactly the question you would ask Jesus: "Don't you care?"

If you care, then why did you allow us to get in this boat? Why did you allow us to buy this house? Move to this town? Take this job? Get married?

If you care, you wouldn't be sleeping. Don't you care that we're drowning? In debt? In bitterness? In loneliness? In disappointment? If you care, then you'd do something.

Peter and the other disciples struggle to believe that God cares, because they're doing what we often do—measuring God's concern for us by how hard it's raining.

Transfer the Weight

"Cast your anxiety on God."

When I see the word *cast* in Peter's writing, my mind immediately connects it to fishing. Peter's a fisherman, right? He's using his own career lingo to describe what we need to do with our anxieties.

If that's what he's saying, it's a little discouraging, because in fishing you cast the line out and then you reel it back in. It's always coming right back to you. So that idea is a nonstarter. As it happens, the word *cast* isn't a fishing term. It's used one other time in Scripture, and it's translated as "transfer" or, even more literally, "transfer the weight."

Sometimes people talk about just letting your anxiety go. You've been hanging on to all these worries and concerns. Just open up your hands and release your anxiety. But if you are in the gym, laying down on a bench holding up the weighted bar, letting go is not great advice. If you just release the weight, it's going to come crashing down on you.

Peter doesn't say simply to release it; he says to *transfer* it. Let God carry the weight that has been holding you back and keeping you down.

Different Weights

What are you holding on to that you need to transfer over to God? Anxieties—let's raise them cautiously. Taking inventory of anxiety items makes us anxious. So let's try it this way—instead of being specific, I'll stick to broad categories.

The unknown

So much of the anxiety that seems to paralyze us and keep us from moving forward revolves around the what-ifs.

What if there's another terrorist attack? What if there's a shooting at my child's school? What if the economy collapses? What if I never find someone to spend my life with? What if I can't get pregnant? What if I do get pregnant? What if our marriage doesn't make it? What if I don't get accepted?

Sören Kierkegaard wrote a small book called *The Concept of Anxiety*. There's one line in there that always pops up in psychology and philosophy classroom discussions: "Anxiety is the dizziness of freedom."[3]

For the record, he's not talking about the kind of freedom we mean when we talk about our freedom in Christ—freedom from guilt and sin doesn't make us anxious. Kierkegaard is referring to the freedom of possibilities in life, those times when we have so many choices we stall out. Our head is spinning with possibilities. We wish Jesus would show up and tell us what to do.

Instead, he tells us what *not* to do. "Do not worry about tomorrow, for tomorrow will worry about itself. Each day has enough trouble of its own" (Matt. 6:34). A lot of our anxieties fall under the category of *tomorrow*. That's where we can lose ourselves in the dizziness of possibilities.

Christ tells us, "Don't go there." Those worries will keep, so stay put in the moment. This alone dramatically decreases the worry inventory.

The unlikely

Similarly, some of what is known is possible but incredibly unlikely. We live in a world of twenty-four-hour news. We now have the ability to learn about catastrophes almost the second they happen—no more waiting to be saddened by events.

These days you don't even have to turn on a television. The updates come directly to your phone. My phone is constantly sending me alerts of things that are going wrong for other people around the world. There needs to be an off button for "Anxiety Alerts."

"For with much wisdom comes much sorrow; the more knowledge, the more grief" (Eccles. 1:18). Today, we can grieve in high tech.

But what if our anxiety is based on somebody's fib?

The phrase "fake news" became popular in 2017. Facebook took a lot of heat for not properly vetting and regulating news that was actually fake. I compiled some of the fake news headlines that millions of people read.

- *Charles Manson to be released on parole in Johnson City, Tennessee.* That doesn't make me very anxious. Do you know why? Because I don't live in Johnson City. If I did, then suddenly everyone would look a little like Charles Manson.
- *Weapon-toting clowns go on murderous rampage.* For a few months, there was national anxiety over dangerous clowns roaming the streets at night. Which led to another fake news story.
- *Congress passes law authorizing citizens to legally shoot and kill suspicious clowns.* From my perspective, any clown not at a circus is suspicious. Stay on your turf, clowns.
- *Elderly woman accused of training her sixty-five cats to steal from the neighbors.* Now you can feel anxious

when a stray cat wanders onto your property. What's your neighbor lady been up to? This could crack the case of the missing TV remote.

It's all fake news, but if we believe it, the anxiety is real enough.

The uncontrollable

Most of our anxiety comes from situations and people we don't control. An expert in the field of stress, Dr. Edward Hallowell, gives this equation for anxiety: "A heightened sense of vulnerability and a diminished sense of power."[4] You're on a battlefield without armor or weaponry. High risk, no recourse.

When I read that equation, I think about teaching my youngest daughter to drive. She's doing okay. Although on occasion, she gets her rights and lefts mixed up. Which can be ~~problematic~~ terrifying.

Sitting in the passenger's seat while she's behind the wheel is the definition of a heightened sense of vulnerability and a diminished sense of power. While she drives, I'm on edge. I've got the dashboard in a death grip. I'm constantly slamming on brakes that don't exist. My voice goes up three octaves every time I try to give her instructions. And it's because I don't have control. I feel vulnerable. Maybe that describes how you feel about a relationship, a job situation, or a mission that God has called you to.

You've probably heard of the Serenity Prayer. It's often used to help people in recovery, and it goes like this: "God, grant me the serenity to accept the things I cannot change, the courage to change the things I can, and the wisdom to know the difference."[5] That last part is where the anxiety seeps in—not knowing the difference.

Maybe you feel anxious about finances. There are some things about your financial situation that you can change but other things you can't. Maybe you feel anxious about your health. There are some things you can control about it but other things you can't. It's all in discerning the difference.

What about a relationship that has you feeling anxious? You think, *If I could just control how this person would respond, then I would have peace in my life.* It even seems as if trying to push the needle forward on their feelings has the opposite effect you want. You move closer, they back away. Then the more they back away, the harder you push forward. And the more anxious you become. Worry-based action creates more worry.

Whatever your brand of anxiety, Peter makes it clear you're taking on even more weight as you try to run a competitive race. You're slowing down, panting, giving up. God wants you to travel light and get there faster.

Different Ways of Casting

Take a minute and ask yourself this question: *How do I deal with the anxiety I feel?*

In an article called "Surviving Anxiety," Scott Stossel shares some of his journey in dealing with anxiety. He writes:

Here's what I've tried to deal with my anxiety: individual psychotherapy, family therapy, group therapy, cognitive-behavioral therapy, rational emotive behavior therapy, acceptance and commitment therapy, hypnosis, meditation, role-

playing, exposure therapy, massage therapy, self-help work-
books, prayer, acupuncture, yoga, Stoic philosophy, and
audiotapes I ordered off a late-night TV infomercial. And
medication. Lots of medication. Thorazine. Imipramine. De-
sipramine. Nardil. BuSpar. Prozac. Zoloft. Paxil. Wellbutrin.
Effexor. Lexapro. Cymbalta. Luvox. Trazodone. Levoxyl. In-
deral. Serax. Centrax. St. John's wort. Zolpidem. Librium.
Klonopin. Valium. Ativan. Xanax. Also: beer, wine, gin,
bourbon, vodka, and scotch. Here's what's worked: nothing.[6]

Please don't hear me putting down medication and professional help; for some people on the anxiety spectrum, those
things are appropriate. But I do worry that more and more,
we turn to popping a pill, taking a drink, watching porn,
or shopping as a quick fix when we should be casting our
anxiety on God.

In his book *High Society*, Joseph Califano has some thoughts
in this direction. At the time of writing, he was the chairman
of the National Center on Addiction and Substance Abuse at
Columbia University. Califano says:

> Chemistry is chasing Christianity as the nation's largest re-
> ligion. Indeed, millions of Americans who, in times of per-
> sonal crisis and emotional and mental anguish, once turned
> to priests, ministers, and rabbis for keys to the heavenly king-
> dom, now go to physicians and psychiatrists, who hold the
> keys to the kingdom of pharmaceutical relief, or to drug
> dealers and liquor stores, as chemicals and alcohol replace
> the confessional as a source of solace and forgiveness.[7]

Peter doesn't mention pills or priests or psychiatrists. He
says to cast our anxiety on God. But that's a little vague,

isn't it? How exactly does one go about doing something like that?

Context helps. People tend to quote this Bible verse as a stand-alone statement of inspiration. But we need to add in the verse just preceding 1 Peter 5:7 to get a clue here:

> Humble yourselves, therefore, under God's mighty hand, that he may lift you up in due time. Cast all your anxiety on him because he cares for you. (1 Pet. 5:6–7)

The New International Version translates the two verses into two separate sentences, putting a period between the two when it should be a comma. So the "cast your anxiety" portion is actually the back end of a complete thought. Let's try reading it this way, to get the key segments together:

> Humble yourselves . . . casting your anxiety on him.

This changes things, doesn't it? We humble ourselves *by* casting our anxieties on him. But it goes the other way too: when we cast our anxieties on him, we humble ourselves. Peter is making a connection that can be elusive: pride and anxiety. Let's unpack a few ways that pride can make us anxious.

Pride makes me self-centered.

The more self-centered I am, the more I'm concerned about my own pleasures, desires, and comfort. The more I focus on those things, the more anxious I'm going to feel.

Think about our current culture's obsession with social media. It can be an amazingly efficient tool for so much: staying up-to-date with family, reconnecting with old friends, and networking for jobs, just to name a few. But there's quite a bit of research coming out about how the rise of social media coincides with an epidemic rise in anxiety.

Why? It causes us to obsess about our lives, our image, and how others perceive us. Constantly taking selfies throughout the day isn't a helpful antidote for anxiety. Social media has a way of reinforcing anxiety, because it causes us to ruminate on what other people think or what we're missing out on. This is increasingly cited as a source of anxiety for teenagers and young adults, called FOMO (fear of missing out). We feel anxious when we see things our friends are doing together, without us. Twenty-four hours a day, we can be reminded of what we're missing.

Pride refuses to ask for help.

So much of our anxiety results from the refusal to humble ourselves and ask God—or anyone else—for help. We feel like giving up because we've insisted on carrying the weight on our own. Think about some anxiety you're dealing with and ask yourself, *Have I asked anyone to help me?*

My wife's little brother, Vince, and his family recently moved to Louisville, which is also our home. This is great, except that, to be honest, he's a little annoying. He's annoying because he's good at a lot of things I'm not.*

Vince likes to build, fix, and repair things that need to be built, fixed, and repaired. As if that's not annoying enough, he actually enjoys manual labor. I understand manual labor is sometimes necessary, and I'm not afraid of a little dirt

* I think we can all agree that people who do things better than we do are highly irritating.

and sweat, but when someone *enjoys* manual labor? To me, that's a red flag.

Now that Vince lives close to us, I'm beginning to hear certain suggestions from my wife, such as, "Hey, why don't you call my brother and ask for help?" Trim needs to be replaced. The garage door isn't working. A sink isn't draining properly. "Why don't you call my brother and ask for help?"

After ignoring that question for the umpteenth time, I stopped and asked myself, *Say, why* don't *I ask him for help?*

It's not because he would mind; he'd probably enjoy it. Yep, annoying. The reason I don't ask for help is simple: pride. The things that need to get done around the house are causing anxiety in my life, and if I transferred the weight of those things over to Vince, I would feel a lot better. But saying to another guy, "I need help. Would you help me?" is not a task where I excel. I'm better at replacing trim.*

It's one thing when I refuse to ask for help with fixing a garage door, but sometimes I've needed help to be a better husband, a better father, or a better pastor, and I haven't been able to say the words, "I need help. Would you help me?"

Maybe that's true for some of the anxiety you're dealing with. Maybe there's a lot of stress right now in your home because of problems in your marriage. Things have been that way for a while. Have you asked anyone for help? Have you gotten on your knees and humbled yourself before God and asked for his help? Don't think of it as an admission of defeat. Think of it as anxiety transference.

As a pastor, I often see couples who have quit on their marriage and nobody saw it coming. Friends and family didn't

---

* That's a guess. I've never tried to replace trim.

even know they were having problems. They're giving up on their marriage though they never went to counseling. They've lived with the stress and pressure for so long, they've stumbled under the load and want to give up.

But what if they'd asked for help six months earlier, when they first started fighting over finances? What if he'd asked for help and accountability when he first started having feelings for his coworker? If only they'd humbled themselves and shifted that weight to a sturdier base before it became too heavy.

Maybe your finances are causing a lot of anxiety in your life because of some poor decisions you've made along the way. You should have asked for help a long time ago, but you didn't. Things have gotten worse, which makes it even harder to ask for help, even though you need it more than ever. Chances are, you have some people in your life who would want to help you. It's just that you can't bring yourself to ask.

Pride has control issues.

We talked about an anxiety that comes from the uncontrollable, but why would controlling bring so much anxiety? Because of pride. Pride makes demands and keeps us awake at night going over them. Yet humility acknowledges that our control is limited. It surrenders those things to God. Pride tries to take control; humility trusts that God cares and is capable and transfers the weight over to him.

Pride makes me defensive, so I become really anxious when I feel unfairly criticized.

99

Pride makes me selfish, so I feel anxious when I don't get my way.

Pride makes me stubborn, so I get anxious when someone won't agree with me.

Pride makes me jealous, so I become anxious when someone else has success or passes me up.

Pride makes me critical, so I get anxious if someone else doesn't realize what they are doing wrong or what they need to do differently.

Peter understands how this works. He says to cast our anxiety on God by coming humbly before him. How? The first and greatest step is what we just did: making the connection—acknowledging and confessing the pride and its damage. That's very humbling.

When we worship, we humble ourselves. Worship is a powerful antidote to anxiety because worship and worry aren't compatible with each other. They can't coexist. When we worship God, we are reminded of his greatness and power, and we naturally begin to cast the weight of our anxieties on him.

When we pray and ask God for help, we do just that. Paul writes, "Do not be anxious about anything, but in every situation, by prayer and petition, with thanksgiving, present your requests to God. And the peace of God, which transcends all understanding, will guard your hearts and your minds in Christ Jesus" (Phil. 4:6–7).

He doesn't just tell us to pray about it; he tells us *how* to pray. Prayer that casts the weight of anxiety on God is prayer that is full of thanksgiving and supplication.

Telling Our Anxieties

Have you ever tried to pray about your anxiety, then, a few minutes in, you feel the anxiety increase? You think to yourself, *This isn't working.*

That's because in our prayers we often tell God about our anxieties but never get around to telling our anxieties about God. When our prayers are filled with thanksgiving, we are telling our anxieties what we have to be thankful for. Anxiety has a way of blinding us to God's blessings, but thanksgiving opens our eyes. It's a proactive way of attacking anxieties.

When our prayers are filled with supplication, meaning that we make our requests known to God, we are telling our anxieties that God is on our side and can carry the weight.

David models this for us in his psalms. If you read through that book, you'll notice how there is often a shift in his prayers. He might begin by talking about the reasons he has to be anxious: his enemies are chasing him. His life is in danger. The guilt of his sin is too heavy.

But then there's a shift. It happens in virtually every psalm. David stops telling God about his anxieties and starts telling his anxieties about God: *God can defeat my enemies. God can rescue me from danger. God can take away the guilt of my sin.* So many psalms begin in doldrums and end in worship.

For many, casting their anxieties on God is a daily process. I asked a young lady in our college ministry to put in her own words how she has learned to tell her anxieties about God.

> If I could describe the past five years of my life in one word, it would be *treacherous*. The trials I experienced led to years of feeling angry and unwanted by everyone around me, but

my biggest enemy just happened to be the one who seemed to be narrating this story. I was at war with myself.

For the past five years of my life, I've struggled with a depression that seems to have taken over every space of my body. I was so broken and weak, I couldn't even bend down to pick up the pieces of my heart and give them to the One everyone around me was saying could heal me. Healing didn't seem possible, not on those long nights when I finally fell asleep on my tear-soaked pillow, wishing I'd cease to exist in the morning.

I thought this was my new reality for the rest of my life, and I was ready to give up.

Although the past five years have been brutal, I've learned so much about the Lord that I would have never even thought about if I hadn't walked through this dark season. I learned that even though I can't control the circumstances around me, I know the One who can.

I thought I would have to spend the rest of my days crying in my bed because there was nothing else in this world for me. But this pit I was in turned out to be the place where I learned the most about myself and who my Father is. I learned to be faithful in prayer even when it felt like God was not listening to the desperate prayers of this child. I learned that God is faithful even when he seems nowhere to be found, that he's present even when I push him away out of frustration.

I was ready to give up, but God's stubborn love refused to let me go. My God is who he says he is, and that is enough for me to cling to today and every day.

I still have tough days where it's as if my depression has won the fight yet again. But God gently reaches his hand down and reminds me this isn't a battle I'm fighting alone. He wipes my tears and reminds me that he has already won the battle. Even when I cannot see because of those tears, I know he is faithfully pursuing my heart, and that's enough to set my soul at peace. I haven't given up because I know that I have a faithful Father on my side who will never give up on me.

Listen to me—God is fighting for you. The God of the universe will help you stand again. He cares how you feel; you are not alone. If you're struggling with depression, remember that God is close to the brokenhearted and that weeping lasts for the night, but joy comes in the morning. Don't give up.

Don't just tell God about your anxieties; tell your anxieties about God. I get that some of you might be thinking, *You don't understand my weight. It's too much. No one can carry it.* Or maybe you're thinking, *It's heavy for me and wearing me down, but it's not a big enough deal to bother God.*

But that's like me telling you, when you sprain your ankle, just to be grateful you didn't break your leg. Pain is pain. Weight is weight. I'm not worried about comparing it, and neither is God. He doesn't weigh our prayers on a worry scale.

Please hear me. The weight you carry isn't part of who God made you and formed you to be in the beginning. You are his loved one whom he adores. He sees you in your struggle, your brokenness, and even your pride-induced anguish. His heart aches because yours does, and he's moved to tenderness and compassion. He desires to take your weight from you. He desires you unhindered. He desires you free.

What weight do you need to transfer over to God? "Cast all your anxiety on him because he cares for you" (1 Pet. 5:7). The power of this verse came to life for me a number of years ago. Back when my son was four, we were on a family road trip.[8] We'd been driving through the night before finally stopping at a hotel to catch a little sleep before finishing the trip the next day.

I was unloading a few things from the trunk when my son came around back to get his bag. He was barely awake, and when I handed it to him, it almost pulled him to the ground. The two of us began to walk across the parking lot toward the hotel. After a few steps, he stopped and looked as if he couldn't go any farther. I said, "Hey buddy, can I carry that for you?"

I knew he wanted to do it himself, but he was so tired. He reluctantly nodded. I grabbed his bag and threw it over my shoulder. It didn't even seem like extra weight.

I started to walk toward the hotel, but when I turned and looked over my shoulder, I noticed my son was still standing in the parking lot looking exhausted. I walked back to him and said, "You coming, buddy?" He said, "Dad, will you carry me too?"

I scooped him up in my arms, happy to carry his weight. Happy to carry him. I carried the weight of my son and his baggage, and it was more of a joy than a task.

If the load you are carrying has become too heavy, if the anxieties of this life have weighed you down, if you're tired and ready to give up—God sees the load you carry and the weight you're under, and he asks, "Why don't you let me carry that for you?"

5

Unchained from Religion

I have learned about a phenomenon that happens some-times with prisoners who are incarcerated for a significant period of time. They have a hard time adjusting to life on the outside when they are released. They get so accustomed to prison and the way things work behind bars that living free can feel uncomfortable and overwhelming to them. They are set free, but they don't know how to live free. The word for this is *institutionalization*.

There's a scene in the movie *The Shawshank Redemption* that defines it perfectly. Most of the movie takes place within the walls of a prison. Red, played by Morgan Free-man, explains to the other inmates this idea of being insti-tutionalized (please read in your best Morgan Freeman voice for full effect):

> I am telling you, these walls are funny. First you hate them; then you get used to them. Enough time passes and you get so you depend on 'em. It doesn't mean you like 'em. It doesn't

even mean you want 'em. But you get used to 'em, and then enough time passes and you depend on 'em.[1]

"Prisoner" can set in as an identity like any other. It can come to define people. And when these prisoners are set free, they no longer know who they are. As Red shows in the movie, some will be tempted to commit some petty crime just to violate probation and get sent back inside those walls, where life is neatly defined. Where decisions are cut and dried.

First-century Christians experienced something like that. Jesus had come to set them free from the weight of religion and the burden of the law. They were free to run the race without the chains of religion holding them back. But many of them had been institutionalized and were choosing to live under its weight.

Hebrews 12:1–3 challenges us to throw off all the extra weight—everything that hinders—as we run the race of life. And we saw that *hinders* can mean any kind of weight.

Anxiety is obvious dead weight. It's a pleasure to throw it off, once we figure out how. But I'm thinking about another kind of dead weight, one that disguises itself as "good weight." Why would anyone throw off the weight of religion? How can religion ever be described as a weight?

Let's clarify our terms. When I say *religion*, I'm talking about a system that emphasizes rules, rituals, and regulations as a way to earn God's favor. Throughout world history, civilizations have designed various religions in this way, because there was always the desire to get God to do for people what they couldn't do for themselves: give rain to the crops, win a battle against another tribe, drive out a plague. Religions can be attempts to barter with God. Or maybe just to stack ourselves up against each other.

In Western culture, some of us have grown up with this weight attached to us. The message of religion was always to try harder, to do better. I talked to a guy after church one weekend who had been raised under this weight. Eventually he could no longer bear the load, and in college he decided to be done with it. He was fine for a while, then life took a few sharp turns and he found himself in the deep down dark. He began coming back to church.

I was visiting with him after a service one weekend, and he was telling me about the religious experience he'd had while growing up. He said, "Every time I went to church, the message I heard was, 'Thanks for playing. Try again next week.'"

I'd never heard it put that way, but it made sense. Every week, he felt like he wasn't trying hard enough to be good enough in an elusive game with rules that weren't always clear and were constantly being added to. No wonder he buckled under the pressure. He wasn't getting anywhere under that load.

For some of you, this idea is confusing. You grew up thinking that religion was the track for running the race God set out for you. But Jesus spoke of religion as a weight—as an actual part of the problem instead of a technique for running.

In Matthew 23, a group of religious leaders listens to Jesus teach. These leaders are known as the best and brightest of their day, the most spiritual people around. They know the Scriptures backward, forward, and sideways, and they define for everyone else what the daily rules are. Their religious résumés are impressive. Everybody but Jesus defers to them. He isn't having it, though. He delivers a fairly stinging rebuke in the form of a sermon.

A significant issue that Jesus addresses is their practice of loading people up with excess rules and regulations. He says of them, "They crush people with unbearable religious demands and never lift a finger to ease the burden" (Matt. 23:4 NLT).

Jesus Is Better

Religion does that. It crushes people under the weight of trying hard enough to be good enough, and it does nothing to ease the burden. Jesus got that point across, and Paul wrote letters and formed churches where that point became clear. Good works alone never brought anyone any closer to God.

But the readers of Hebrews had a difficult time throwing off the weight of long tradition in these teachings. So much of the book of Hebrews is about that very subject—reconciling the Jesus who wrote the law with the Jesus who finally completes it, answers it, and removes its burden once and for all.

The law got one thing done: it dramatically played out the futility of our trying to please God. But Jesus offers his work of perfection as our own. He who kept the law impeccably perfectly intercedes for the rest of us who can't.

And his intercession on our behalf is a free gift of grace. We need only ask.

Think of it this way. The Olympics offer pole vaulting—the powerful jump over a high bar. Think of that bar as the law, and Christ as the only hero who has ever cleared it—then he assigns his achievement, his medal, his full reward to us. All of us have been required to line up and make the leap. All of us have been told we must clear the bar. And nobody else has made it very far off the ground at all; we've all ended up in the dirt, humiliated. "Thanks for playing. Try again next week." Until one man cleared it.

A major theme of Hebrews is the superiority of Christ. That's the case that its writer has been making. Another way we could say this is simply *Jesus is better.* Fix your eyes on Jesus, because Jesus is better; he is superior to everything and everyone else.

The words translated as "better" and "superior" show up fifteen times in the book of Hebrews. The original readers would have mostly been first-generation Jewish Christians. They were facing persecution for their faith, and culturally they were being ridiculed and opposed. So the message that "Jesus is better" was a message given to encourage them *not* to go back, *not* to give up.

If you read through Hebrews, you can make a list of everything that Jesus is better than. Jesus is better than the law. Jesus is better than traditions. Jesus is better than the prophets of old.

The first verses of Hebrews point out that in the past, God spoke through the prophets, but now he has spoken to us through his Son. Then chapter 3 makes the case that "Jesus is better than Moses." This would have been offensive to many of its original readers.*

You didn't mess with the name of Moses. He was the ultimate prophet. But Hebrews makes it clear that it's not even a close contest. Moses was a servant and Jesus is the master. The list keeps going: Jesus is better than the angels.

---

* Like some middle schoolers trying to tell me that Lonzo Ball is better than Michael Jordan.

Jesus is better than the high priests. Jesus is better than the old covenant. Jesus is better than the sacrificial system. Don't trade freedom in Christ for the weight of religion. Jesus is better than religion.

Jesus is just better. Always has been, always will be.

Institutionalized

Choosing to strain under the weight of the law rather than running free with Jesus was a challenge for many of the New Testament churches. This was something new and exciting, but thousand-year habits are hard to break. Many of the believers would become confused and slide back to the old religious ways, because it was all they'd really known.

Religion is attractive because it offers a pecking order, a set standard. There is something very appealing about a system that lets you measure how good you are. The religious leaders Jesus was speaking of in Matthew 23 were partly made of a group called the Pharisees. If there was a championship team for religious people, that would be the Phightin' Pharisees. They'd have made sure their name was on the front of their jersey instead of the back. They were proud. They'd developed an exhaustive list of rules, dos and don'ts that far exceeded what was taught in the Hebrew law.

There were more than six hundred rules in the Old Testament—not nearly enough for the Pharisees. They found ways to "clarify" the fine points. If God gave one commandment, they'd come up with one hundred ways to make sure it was fully obeyed. Each rule was another weight on the runner's back.

God said to honor the Sabbath day by keeping it as a holy day of rest. But this *honor* thing—how do we know what constitutes it? The Pharisees were on it. They decided and decreed that:

I. A person could only walk seven-tenths of one mile on the Sabbath.

II. If you got off your donkey, you weren't allowed to take off your saddle; that would be working.

III. If a hen laid an egg on the Sabbath, you were not allowed to eat the egg, because the hen had worked on the Sabbath.

Can you see how such an approach could be burdensome? They created a list of rules and rituals, then they kept track. They probably published weekly standings for holiness.

The point was, there was a well-established way to feel better about yourself and more judgmental of others.

That was then, this is—the same, sadly. We have plenty of examples of how that tradition carries on, because it's not a Hebrew thing; it's a human thing. People come to church and we hand out weights. They spend the week trying to run under them.

The Bible teaches that we should dress modestly. No argument there. But somebody made rules so we wouldn't have to wonder. "Ladies, you can't wear pants; you have to wear dresses—which can't be tight. And they can't be more than the width of a dollar bill above your knee."

The Bible teaches that we should not let any unwholesome talk come out of our mouths. But which words, exactly?

Acceptable and unacceptable words are somehow ratified and legislated.

Now it's not just bad words you can't say, it's words that *sound* like bad words. Not only is it wrong to take the Lord's name in vain but it's wrong to say *by gosh* or *good golly*.*

The Bible teaches us to guard our hearts, and we follow that with all kinds of subclauses and provisos and codicils. Such as, "Thou shall not watch R-rated movies," or "Thou shall not listen to secular music."

You could add to the list. It does change over time, but for rule afficionados, revising and amending the rules is half the fun of religion.

Religion gives us a feeling of superiority, much like the guy at the gym who walks in wearing a string tank top and using a gallon jug as his water bottle. He adds more and more weight to the bar, then grunts loud enough that everyone in the gym can see how much he can lift, bro.

A religious leader is found doing this in Luke 11. Jesus is eating at the home of a Pharisee, and we're told that Jesus didn't wash his hands before the meal. That was one of the many laws the religious leaders had come up with and held over the people. Jesus not washing his hands before the meal is not an accidental oversight. He knows what he's doing. He's picking a fight with the guy in the string tank top. It's about time.

When the religious leader notices, he basically says to Jesus, "The Lord has told us to wash our hands." Maybe Jesus is tempted to say, "No, I don't think I ever said it exactly like that."

---

* Other words too close to the real thing for the truly elite to say: *darn*, *dang*, *doggonnit*, and the particularly nefarious *dagnabit*. You know you want to say it.

But Jesus makes a point that he's not okay with all their extra rules and add-ons. He goes on to basically accuse the religious leaders of being bullies who use religion as a way to promote themselves and control people. And Jesus wasn't going to stand for it, because the weight of all this religion crushes the people.

Think of how we do this. In religious circles, we have what amounts to invisible religious merit badges. We try to show them off nonchalantly. "Here's my never been drunk badge." "Here's my technically never had sex before marriage badge." "Here's my expert evangelism badge." "Here's my consistent quiet time badge." "Here's my perfect family badge."*

Of course, we can't actually point out these badges, or we might be asked to give back our "humility badge," which is one of our favorites to show off. Instead, we try to work our accomplishments casually into conversations and look down condescendingly on others who are still in the religious Cub Scouts.

The Pharisees turned holiness into a religious weightlifting competition, and people were getting crushed. These religious leaders were supposed to be shepherds who keep the flock safe, but they had become the neighborhood bullies, picking on the wounded and piling on the weak.

Jesus came to take the weight of religion off us. The law of sin and death can no longer hold us down. I love the way *The Message* paraphrases the words of Jesus:

> Are you tired? Worn out? Burned out on religion? Come to me. Get away with me and you'll recover your life. I'll

* Which you can only achieve by convincing everyone on social media that it's true.

show you how to take a real rest. Walk with me and work with me—watch how I do it. Learn the unforced rhythms of grace. I won't lay anything heavy or ill-fitting on you. Keep company with me and you'll learn to live freely and lightly. (Matt. 11:28–29)

Jesus came to free us from the weight of trying hard enough to be good enough. I can keep on playing by those rules, since it's all I was taught. But if I do, several things will happen—none of them good.

Broadly speaking, I'll continue living in some ugly form of pride, wrapped in pretty paper to look like righteousness. But more specifically, there are four distinct experiences that tend to surface when I try to run while shouldering the weight of religion. It's easy to see how these experiences cause us to give up.

1. I'll grow frustrated.

There's nothing more frustrating than trying to do something you aren't capable of doing. Imagine being taken out to the pole vault bar when you were a kid. Somebody would say, "See that bar up there? The world record is more than twenty feet. Nobody has ever topped that. But we've set the bar a few inches higher than the world record, because we feel you need to be *perfect*. You need to get over that bar or you've failed."

Then the coach leaves you to it. He can't help you toward that goal, because he can't make that leap either. He has no clue. Everybody you know spends their lives running with that pole, stabbing it into the ground, and trying to jump—only to end up eating dirt.

That would be a frustrating way to live. Your whole life would be built around attempting to do something nobody anywhere can do.

This is what makes religion so frustrating. It bases life on impossible standards, makes you feel guilty for missing them, and leaves you powerless to do anything about it.

2. I'll feel exhausted.

It's not just frustrating; it's tiring to try harder and harder only to feel like you can never make it. You're aching from hitting the ground time after time. You have bruises. You feel dirty. And looking up, you see the bar continuing to tower over you.

Just because your fatigue is real doesn't mean the struggle is worth it—or even valid for that matter. Who even said life is about pole-vaulting? Couldn't it have been about the marathon race? Beach volleyball? Meat loaf cooking?

Who makes these rules?

3. I'll act fake until I can't fake it anymore.

After a while, the people sitting in the dirt, beneath the height of the bar, realize they can't go on this way. To admit that every single person in the world is an utter failure would be unthinkable. So there's an unspoken agreement to *pretend*. People begin claiming they made that jump five minutes ago, just before you got here. Or they could do it if they wanted; they're just practicing the running-with-the-pole part right now. Or they start evaluating who has the nicest gym shorts or shoes. They keep building new measurements.

Soon there's a six-inch-thick manual on pole-vaulting, even though no one has ever succeeded at it.

That's how religion works. I'll put on a good show, and people will look at me or scroll through my social media and think I'm making it happen. Since religion puts the emphasis on what others think, then as long as I can keep up the performance, I'm good. But pretending to be someone you're not becomes exhausting.

4. I'll end up conceited or defeated.

When it's about trying harder, it will always lead to comparisons. We will look around at other people and compare ourselves, feeling either pride or failure. We'll compare down and feel conceited or compare up and feel defeated.

Either way, it's just a matter of time until we become discouraged and quit or prideful and fall. Both outcomes keep us from running the race that God has marked out for us.

FOWOT

One of the ways Jesus sets us free from the weight of religion is by setting us free from fear of what other people think. In Matthew 23, just after Jesus says that the religious leaders crush people with the unbearable weight of religious demands, he says of them in verse 5, "Everything they do is done for people to see."

The weight of what other people think is one that religious people tend to carry everywhere they go. If you grew up under the weight of religion, you know how much emphasis is put on the outside. Jesus tells the religious leaders in Matthew 23 that they may look good on the outside, and everyone may be impressed, but they are like whitewashed tombs. On the outside they are clean and well-manicured, but on the inside is a rotting corpse.

The religious leaders never particularly enjoyed that word picture.

Let me give you a few indicators that you might be living with the fear of what others think (FOWOT):

You go along with what someone else wants but secretly resent it.

You change your opinion based on what everyone else thinks.

You are afraid of being seen as weird after voicing an idea.

You read into what other people say or do.

You have a hard time asking for help.

You have a difficult time saying no.

You are critical of others.

Understanding how God thinks of us sets us free from FOWOT. Once we see ourselves through his eyes we become much less concerned with how we look in the eyes of others. The good news of the gospel is that Jesus makes us clean. Not only does he take away our sin but he gives us righteousness so that we stand before God without blemish or defect. That's how he sees us. Maybe you grew up being taught that God would love you more if you did something or if you didn't do something. Some of you attend church every week because you think God will love you more if you go to church. That gets you on the game board. Then there are bonus God's Love Points for putting 10 percent of your money in the offering plate as it goes by. Maybe a few more God's Love Points for reading your Bible during the week.

God doesn't love that way. His love would actually be so much easier to understand if it was conditional and performance-based. It's hard for us to accept, but the truth is God doesn't love you more if you've never been addicted to drugs or if you've never slept around or if you've never had an abortion. He doesn't love you more than the people who have done all those things. He doesn't love you more because you dress modestly or because you give generously. He doesn't love you more because you scored the most points on the team, or because you sing the solos, or because you're a great leader, or because you're a gifted teacher.

You are free from earning God's love. When you begin to understand his love and acceptance, it releases you from fearing what other people think. Then, when you are finally free from the heavy weight of that, you feel light and swift, ready to sprint, eager to get back up and fulfill the mission purpose of your life.

On a return trip from Haiti, our family's flight was delayed. My oldest daughter had invited a friend to join us, so there were seven of us trying to get home. I knew our connecting flight in Miami was going to be tight. When we landed, we sat on the runway, waiting for our gate to open up.

I was doing the math. We had less than an hour until our flight home to Louisville would take off. I knew there was almost no chance we'd make it. We had to get through customs, get our bags, recheck them, go back through security, and make it to our connecting gate.

We got to customs, and the line was going to take several hours. People all around us were frustrated. My wife said to me, "You should say something to one of the security workers. Maybe they'll let us cut through since our flight is getting ready to take off."

I couldn't do that. What would everyone think? They *all* had to wait.

A few minutes passed. Again she said to me, "You need to do something."

I was ready to give up on any chance of making it and accept defeat. She reminded me that if we didn't make the flight, we'd be getting on a shuttle, cramming into a hotel room, then coming back to the airport in the morning in hopes of getting seven seats on another flight. We have this weird thing in our marriage where she points out something I should do again and again until I finally do it.*

I said, "Follow me."

The seven of us rushed up to a security guard and desperately asked if we could cut in line. He looked at our tickets and said, "You'll never make it." But he let us cut to the front. As the guy was checking our passports, he said, "You guys need to run as fast as you can."

I like to run from time to time. But I haven't run at the "fast as I can" setting since I was in high school. It wasn't impressive; it was disturbing. Some people pointed and stared. Others looked away, embarrassed for me. We got our bags checked back in, and now our flight was boarding. But we still had to get back through security.

In the security line, about twenty people were in front of us. My wife said, "You need to say something."

I took a deep breath and did it. A little embarrassed, I yelled at the security guard that our flight was boarding and asked if

* That's probably just us.

we could cut to the front. He told us to ask all the people in front of us. I was drenched in sweat and had a look of panic in my eyes as I asked the twenty people in front of us if we could cut in front of them. Remarkably, they all said yes.*

My faith in humanity was restored. We got through security, and once again we ran in a dead sprint through the airport. I was making high-pitched beeping noises like the airport shuttle carts, hoping people would get out of our way. I was panting and gasping for air, but we made it to our seats with less than a minute to go before they closed the door on the plane.

Here's my point: I had to come to the realization that either we were going to give up and call it quits, or we weren't going to care what anyone else thought and were going to go for it. Once I decided that I didn't care what the people around me would think, I felt free to run as fast as I could. Once we settle in our minds that we aren't living to impress others or for the applause of this world, we're free to run.

The Galatians were another church group who went back to the simple but impossible system of religious law. There were false teachers who came into the church and began to elevate the religious rules and rituals, and many of the Christians were willing to carry that weight again. In Galatians 2, Paul tries to remind the believers that Jesus has freed them from that burden. Here's how *The Message* paraphrases the end of that chapter:

> I tried keeping rules and working my head off to please God, and it didn't work. So I quit being a "law man" so that I could

---

* There was one lady who said no, but we all pretended we didn't hear her. Just like Jesus would've done.

be *God's* man. Christ's life showed me how, and enabled me to do it. I identified myself completely with him. Indeed, I have been crucified with Christ. My ego is no longer central. It is no longer important that I appear righteous before you or have your good opinion, and I am no longer driven to impress God. Christ lives in me. The life you see me living is not "mine," but it is lived by faith in the Son of God, who loved me and gave himself for me. I am not going to go back on that. (Gal. 2:19–21)

There's so much freedom to be found when we get away from the obsession with what other people think or say. It feels wonderful to stop being someone else's person and to start fitting neatly and perfectly into the personhood God has planned for you.

Why? All people—everyone, you and me included—are faulty, broken, and inconsistent. Why try to depend on the acceptance of others as broken as you?

When we go to God for his gracious approval and loving acceptance, we'll find the greatest freedom ever. You find real freedom and rest and joy when you quit worrying about others' acceptance and just rest in God's.

It's not easy. Everyone around you is just walking. People are telling you you'll never make it. Who cares what they think? When you set the real goal in mind, when you break free, slip the chains, and start running, you realize you just might go farther than you ever dreamed, and to better destinations.

6

Unleashed from Lies

"Don't swim until thirty minutes after eating."

"Why?"

"You'll get cramps. You could drown!"

My mother told me that. I'm guessing your mother told you too. They loved us and wanted to protect us, so they told us not to swim until thirty minutes after eating.* Most of us probably have made that same rule for our children.

Great wisdom.

Except it's not. It's actually not true at all. Swimming after eating will not cause cramps. Your mom meant well, but—and there's no nice way to say this—she lied to you.

I get the feeling you're not convinced. The truth is that wasn't the only lie. You *can* swallow chewing gum.

You protest, "But it will stay in my system for months or years! It can take up to seven years to digest."

You've been lied to. Gum passes through your system at the same rate as anything else you swallow.

* Or ten minutes if your mom didn't love you as much.

123

I understand this is hard to accept. Even after being liberated by the truth, I still panic on the rare occasion I'm forced to swallow gum. Like when communion is being served in church and there is no other option. But the truth is, you can swallow a pack of Big League Chew and go swimming immediately after, and you'll be fine.

The Power of Lies

Most of us believe lies. We don't know they're lies. If we knew they were lies, we wouldn't believe them.

Because we believe lies, we live our lives by them, right? If you believe swimming within thirty minutes of eating is dangerous, you won't do it. And that gives the lie the same power over you as if it were truth. For centuries, people believed the lie that the earth was flat. Because they believed that lie, they wouldn't go too far out in the ocean; they didn't want to fall off the edge.

When you believe a lie, it changes the way you live.

It's obviously not a big deal if you've spent your life avoiding swimming after eating or swallowing chewing gum. But what if you believe more significant lies that have more serious implications?

It's one thing to buy in to the lie that sitting too close to the TV will ruin your eyesight.* But consider the cost of buying in to a lie such as:

You'll never be good enough.

You've made too many mistakes.

* Yep. Mom again.

You'll never be able to stop.

God doesn't really care about you.

No one really cares about you.

If you believe those lies, you will give them tremendous power in your life, because when you believe a lie to be true, you give it the same power as if it were. Believing those lies will make it difficult to keep going. Believing those lies will make you want to give up.

When I went back and read through my notes from all the conversations I had with people in 2017, I was struck by the fact that what was often holding them back and keeping them down was some lie they'd believed. If they kept believing that lie, it would only be a matter of time until they gave up.

If they were going to persevere, to avoid quitting, the lie needed to be exposed. Could it be you've accepted some things to be true that are not true at all? Could it be that those lies are wreaking havoc in your life and are a big part of the reason you feel like giving up?

Leashed and Unleashed

Believing lies has such debilitating and destructive power that our enemy has chosen it as his way of ruining our lives. The Bible teaches us that Satan wants to "steal and kill and destroy" in our lives (John 10:10). How does he do it?

In the garden, Satan's original game plan for ruining Adam and Eve's lives was to get them to believe a lie, as told in Genesis 3. He has been employing that same strategy ever since.

Speaking of Satan, Jesus said, "There is no truth in him. When he lies, he speaks his native language, for he is a liar and the father of lies" (John 8:44). We are told repeatedly that Satan is scheming against us, trying to deceive us and entice us to believe lies. We are warned, "in order that Satan might not outwit us" (2 Cor. 2:11).

We know he's the father of lies, but he has spread too many of them and some are pretty convincing. The alternative is pursuing truth. Jesus said, "I am . . . the truth" (John 14:6) and, "Then you will know the truth, and the truth will set you free" (8:32).

I want to look at some of the lies we commonly believe. Specifically, those that cause us to give up and quit. When I'm trying to encourage someone to keep going or challenging someone to not give up, I know that most of the time they are believing a lie, and that lie needs to be exposed and replaced with God's truth. So let's look at some lies we believe and learn some truths from God that can set us free.

Lie #1: You Don't Have What It Takes

This is one lie that can make us feel like giving up. It comes in a number of variations. Your version might sound more like:

I don't know what I'm doing.
My kids would be better off with a different parent.
No matter how hard I try, it won't be good enough.

This lie says you're not qualified or capable. If you believe it, you will give it the same power as if it were truth, and it won't be long until you give up.

It's interesting, and may be helpful to know, that research indicates that both men and women struggle with feelings of inadequacy, though in different ways. Women tend to blame themselves, assuming they don't have what it takes. Men typically blame their circumstances, believing that someone or something else is at fault. We can all buy into the you-don't-have-what-it-takes lie.

This is an easy lie to believe because there are so many opportunities to compare ourselves nowadays. Everyone puts the best version of themselves on social media. I'm trying to get a petition started that changes the name of Facebook to Façade and Instagram to Mirage. Maybe then we wouldn't look at these airbrushed versions of people's lives and feel so insecure. We compare our normal lives with the highlights of an idealized version of other people's lives, and we feel like we fall short. We start to think we don't have what it takes.

That's not true. It's not true because what you're seeing on social media is mostly not true. Did you know studies have revealed that when someone is having financial struggles, they're more likely to post pictures of themselves spending money? People having marriage issues are more likely to share posts about their romantic dates with their spouse. Why? They want to hide their insecurities. But we see it all and think, *I'm not as good as they are. I don't have what it takes to live a life like that.*

There are consequences for falling into this trap. It can lead to perfectionism. You try to measure up by making everything perfect. Soon you discover perfection is unattainable, so you start feeling guilty, and guilt almost always surfaces in anger.

Then comes fatigue. Now you feel as if you can't keep going, and you're ready to give up. But you feel trapped; you don't know how to quit.

Wanting to quit often leads to escapism. You don't like the way your life makes you feel, so you escape to a romance novel, or Netflix bingeing, or a bottle of wine, or flirtatious texts with someone else, or porn—or staying up half the night playing video games, maybe re-redecorating your house. The list goes on, but it can all be traced back to a lie you believed.

This lie is tricky because there's some truth in it. That's how the best lies work. If a lie was wholly untrue, you'd recognize it and reject it. But there could be some truth to the idea that you don't have what it takes—it's just not the whole truth, and the whole truth is what sets us free. Here it is:

With God, I have everything I need to do everything I need to do.

Would you take a second and read that truth out loud?

Read it aloud again. Stop and spend some time with it. Get to know it a little better. Because this truth is life-changing.

Listen to how this liberating news is shared with us in God's Word: "His divine power has given us everything we need for a godly life" (2 Pet. 1:3). "A godly life" means more than simply a life not dominated by sin. It means God has a great plan for your life and, through his power, will give you everything you need to live it.

So the next time you think you don't have what it takes, reject the lie by saying, "Well, even if that's the case—I know who does have what it takes."

Or try this one: "But he said to me, 'My grace is sufficient for you, for my power is made perfect in weakness'" (2 Cor. 12:9). You may not feel self-sufficient, but his grace is enough. It's all you need.

Another one: "I can do all this through him who gives me strength" (Phil. 4:13). There's nothing you *need* to do that you *can't* do. Through Jesus, it's all possible. When you're weak, it's an opportunity to experience real strength.

Let's read the truth one more time:

With God, I have everything I need to do everything I need to do.

That truth will set you free!

Lie #2: You Can Fix It Yourself

This is another lie that can make us feel like giving up. If we bounce too far in the opposite direction from "You don't have what it takes," we land in the world of "You can fix it yourself." It's the opposite but still a lie—the lie of pride. If we believe it:

We refuse to ask for help, even when help is needed.

We hide our mistakes and weaknesses, even when our only hope for healing is to reveal them.

We think God is unnecessary.

With this self-fix-it lie, the *it* that needs fixing might be a person. Perhaps the person you're trying to fix is your spouse, and you think it's your job to fix "it."

Or maybe you feel like you're raising a couple of little "its." Your job is to repair everything that's out of kilter about them.

Let me ask: If you're trying to fix people, how's that working out for you? Do people like being with you? I'm guessing they're telling you they didn't order a repair person, and now you're both frustrated.

Or the "it" you're trying to fix might be yourself. This is the most common one. You're convinced you can fix your bad habit or addiction or secret sin. You probably haven't seen much progress, but you're still convinced you can fix it on your own.

What you're trying to fix may not be a person but rather a financial situation, or your addiction, or something at your job. Whatever it is, your enemy whispers, *You don't need any help.* That's a lie. When we believe this lie, we try to do it on our own, but often it ends up as a disaster that makes us feel like giving up. We need to ask for help.

When you buy into the lie that you can fix it yourself, a few things happen.

It increases pride.

The Bible says God hates pride, and I'm pretty sure it's because he loves us and hates whatever destroys us. And pride is truly a destroyer. Those who pridefully say, "I don't need any help. I can fix it myself," will find that God is opposing them.

It minimizes legitimate problems.

Believing I can fix it requires me to look at problems unrealistically. If I take the problem seriously and look at it objectively, I'll be forced to realize I can't fix it. But telling myself I'm in control helps me downsize the problem in my mind. Hey, this is no big deal—nothing I can't fix. Reassuring—and dangerous.

It's also why some people have problems with drinking or lust, or spending or anger or marriage. The problem is big, it's bad, and it never goes away. Why? I've minimized it by telling myself it's fixable. "I can quit anytime I want."

It robs intimacy in our relationships.

When I confide in someone and ask for help, it actually deepens the relationship. But if I buy the lie that I can fix it myself, I won't ask anyone for help—and we won't grow closer. I tell myself I don't need anybody.

Admitting to someone else I can't fix it requires vulnerability. I experienced this in my marriage early on; I thought being a man meant I shouldn't need help, so I didn't discuss any of my struggles with my wife. I look back now and realize how deeply I did need my wife's wisdom and discernment. But I robbed myself of that because I didn't want to be vulnerable.

If I had asked for help, three good things would have happened. I would have gotten help, my wife would have felt valued, and we would have drawn closer.

It fuels hypocrisy.

I can't let anyone know how bad things really are in my life, so I have to pretend. I live with this façade, showing the world something too good to be true. Living that way is exhausting. It's not sustainable.

■ ■ ■

This lie, "I can fix it myself," doesn't lead us to the life we want to live. We need to overcome it, and we can because of Jesus. That may sound trite—just the kind of answer you'd expect in a Christian book. But it happens to be powerfully true. In fact, it points to something you may have never realized or understood about Jesus. In Hebrews 4, the writer tells us,

> Therefore, since we have a great high priest who has ascended into heaven, Jesus the Son of God, let us hold firmly to the faith we profess. For we do not have a high priest who is unable to empathize with our weaknesses, but we have one who has been tempted in every way, just as we are—yet he did not sin. (Heb. 4:14–15)

In those days, the high priest was the person who represented you before God. He spoke to God on your behalf, advocated your interests. Jesus is now our high priest, and he understands our weaknesses.

Have you ever thought about the fact that Jesus understands what you go through? Think about his life on earth. He was conceived out of wedlock to a teenage mother, for which he was probably ridiculed by the other kids. He seems to have experienced the death of his earthly father at a relatively young age; he lived in poverty. He was tempted by Satan. One of his closest friends died. He wasn't supported by his family. His friends betrayed and deserted him. He had prayers that seemed to go unanswered.

So what are you struggling with? Whatever it is, Jesus has been there. He doesn't watch from heaven, thinking, *Oh, that seems so horrible.* No, he's experienced what you're experiencing, and he is your representative before God.

So how does that allow us to overcome the I-can-fix-it lie? What does it look like to live by this truth? "Let us then approach God's throne of grace with confidence, so that we may receive mercy and find grace to help us in our time of need" (v. 16).

The command: "Come boldly." I wonder if you need God's help and you're wondering why he's not helping you. The instruction here is *come*, not *wait around*. You need to come to him and to do so boldly. Yes, he is the Lord. Yes, he created everything. But you walk right in there as if you belong—as Jesus says you do. Boldly come to him in your time of need.

It's nothing like applying for a loan in a time of financial need but you're unsure if you're qualified, so you sit nervously in the waiting room, sweating it out, hoping for mercy.

No. He is God, so he has all the power you need, and he finds joy in seeing you grow. He's been where you are, so he understands. And he is for you, so you can trust him completely. As you become vulnerable with him and invite him into your situation, he will begin to redeem it. Tell yourself that truth next time you feel like giving up.

Why try to fix it yourself? You can boldly go to God and find all the help you need. You can bring everything to him because you have a high priest who understands your struggles and who has the power and the desire to help you.

Lie #3: You Deserve to Be Happy

We really, really don't want this one to be a lie. But the fact is, it's not true. And people make decisions based on it all the time.

We see it in the Bible: Eve thought eating the forbidden fruit would make her happy. Cain thought killing Abel would make him happy. Joseph's brothers thought selling him into slavery would make them happy. Samson thought marrying a Philistine would make him happy. David thought sleeping with another man's wife would make him happy. Solomon had 999 women in his life, thinking they'd make him happy, and when they didn't, he thought, *Maybe lucky number one thousand will make me happy.* The rich young ruler thought keeping his wealth would make him happy. Judas thought thirty pieces of silver would make him happy.

We see it today: it's the woman who has been married for twenty-four years but is frustrated because her husband isn't showing her attention. She has reconnected with an old high school boyfriend and has decided to leave her husband. Her reasoning: *Doesn't God want me to be happy?* If that assumption is true, then it justifies leaving her husband. God is saying, *Hey, whatever makes you happy.*

It's the college student who grew up going to church but now feels like he's missing out because everyone else is partying. Finally, he decides he's going to join in. His thinking? *If God loves me, he wants me to have a good time. I mean, doesn't God want me to be happy?*

It's the dating couple who go to church and believe in Jesus but have decided to ignore the "Don't have sex till you're married" thing because God wants them to be "happy."

The most obvious problem is that these decisions don't lead to happiness. The truth is, we've all done things to try to be happy, only to discover they did no such thing.

You may be a little confused right now. You're thinking, *What's wrong with wanting to be happy? Isn't our nation based on the pursuit of happiness? Doesn't God want me to be happy?*

Remember, the best lies mix in a little bit of truth. God loves you. And, like any good parent, he does indeed like you to be happy—but, like any good parent, his ultimate goal for you is not happiness, because he knows there are more important things. He also knows most of your ideas about what will make you happy are wrong.

"God wants me to be happy." It *sounds* as if it should be true. We'd *love* for it to be true. And if it were true, we'd have a clear runway to launch into a life of doing whatever made us happy at that moment. The catch is that short-term happiness nearly always leads to long-term regret.

First, if you believe God wants you to be happy above all else, you'll believe that whatever makes you feel happy must be right and whatever makes you feel unhappy must be wrong. But quite often, the best thing for us turns out to be something that doesn't feel particularly pleasurable at the moment. A physical exam by the doctor won't make me happy at that moment; I'd rather be doing any number of things. What would make me happy, right then, would be to put it off. But it's what I need.

Second, you'll start thinking God exists to serve you and, since happiness is the highest good, God's job is to provide circumstances that make you feel good. But God does not exist to serve you. You exist to serve him.

Third, there's a real chance you'll end up walking away from God. Your circumstances won't change the way you want, you'll blame God for not doing his job of making you happy, and you'll give up on him.

The irony of believing this lie is that people who think they deserve to be happy, and who pursue pleasure as the highest good, tend to be the unhappiest people of all.

When we believe we deserve to be happy, we move on to other lies about finding happiness. For example, we believe happiness is equivalent to the pursuit of pleasure, so we go after things that bring momentary pleasure, sometimes so frantically we hurry past most of the real stuff. We somehow believe happiness is something we pursue. But studies have proven there's no quicker way to be unhappy than making your life about happiness.

This is sometimes called the "pleasure paradox" or the "happiness illusion." The harder you chase after happiness, the more elusive it becomes. It turns out that the pursuit of happiness is the shortcut to misery in a clever disguise.

We think happiness is found by pursuing pleasure, when all the time true happiness is pursuing us in the form of God's love. Think of some of the Bible's great statements about the pursuit of God:

"Take delight in the LORD" (Ps. 37:4).
"Rejoice in the LORD and be glad" (Ps. 32:11).
"Blessed is the people whose God is the LORD" (Ps. 144:15).
"Rejoice in the Lord" (Phil. 4:4).

God wants you to be happy, but it's a happiness that comes from pursuing and knowing him. Unfortunately, people can view God as a means to happiness, believing God will provide them what they need to be happy. No. We don't have God so he can give us blessings to make us happy. We have God, and *he* is ultimate happiness. He is ultimate blessing and joy. Every good gift, every pure happiness, originates in him, so that when we discover he is all that we need, we find a happiness that never runs dry.

Instead of pursuing pleasure, we pursue God, with his promise that if we seek him, we will find him. Happy people don't chase after happiness; they chase after God, and happiness pursues them throughout life.

Wouldn't it be nice if we could finally believe, once and for all, that happiness isn't found by focusing on self? What does it take for us to learn that lesson? God tells us happiness is found in focusing on others. Jesus taught it, modeled it, and showed the ultimate picture of it on the cross. He said that he "did not come to be served, but to serve, and to give his life as a ransom for many" (Matt. 20:28).

It sounds like work. It sounds like a chore, and yet it turns out to be the quickest, surest route to happiness—something as simple as focusing on others. This is the happiness paradox: when people try to make themselves happy, they are more likely to feel depressed, but when they try to make others happy, they are more likely to be happy themselves.

Think about the most joyful people you know. My guess is they're not people who focus on having pleasurable experiences or accumulating money and possessions. I bet the most joyful people you know are people who have learned how to "rejoice in the Lord" and are living by the liberating truth, "The joy of the Lord is [my] strength" (Neh. 8:10). The person you're thinking of made a decision to pursue God, not pleasure, and to focus on others, not themselves.

Happy people are happy not because God gave them the right set of circumstances to be happy. They're happy because God gave them himself, and that makes them happy. They swim in his love today and put their hope in the fact that today is short but eternal life is forever. They know they don't deserve God or heaven, but because of his grace, they have become recipients of an unimaginable gift. And that makes them something even richer than happy: it makes them content.

When things don't go well, sure, it's frustrating; but we remember that we have God, and we've been forgiven, and we're going to heaven forever. And we experience a deeper kind of happiness, not one based on circumstances or feelings but one we have received through God's grace. That truth sets us free and keeps us going when we feel like giving up.

...

It's so easy to be overcome by lies, and those lies can make us feel like giving up. But you can replace those lies with truth. Here's a good one to start you off: God loves you. He finds you so valuable, he paid the price of his Son for you. He wants to give you new life and the power to live it. You have everything you need to have joy and to live a rewarding life. You are never stuck. You can change. In fact, you *are* changing. God is transforming you.

One day God will say, "Enough pain. Enough sorrow. Enough fear. Enough crying." And he will make everything new. On that day, the concept of happiness will cease to exist as a separate condition to have or to lack or to chase. There will be nothing but perfect joy. There will be no unhappiness.

Until then, God offers a world where, if we can navigate past the lies, if we can ground ourselves firmly in truth, happiness is possible. It can be real. It can be deep. It can even be frequent. And it's found only in God, who is always enough.

What lies have you believed? If you knew they were lies you wouldn't believe them, but when lies are believed they have the power of truth over us. If you feel like quitting, ask yourself if there is a lie you are believing. Pray and ask God to reveal any lies you are living by.

7

Untangled from Unbelief

Have you ever walked through a spiderweb? Of course you
have. It's terrifying!

Those things catch you off guard, and three things always
happen. First, you start swiping wildly through the air at
this sticky, invisible mess. You flail around in panic and sheer
disgust.

Then the second thing happens: you remember that wherever there is a spiderweb, there must be a spider! Your casual
flailing turns into frantic and violent brushing, making sure
that there is no possibility a spider has landed on you.

Then the third thing happens: you desperately look around
to see if anyone has been watching. They can't see the spiderweb, just you. And you look insane.

It's the invisibility that makes it so annoying. You never
see it coming.

Life has countless paths, of course, and sticky webs of all
kinds. Which ones have tangled you up? You were moving
forward, running free, and suddenly you ran right into a web.

A coworker gives you a flirtatious look. It seems innocent enough, and it feels good to have someone look at you that way again. You don't mention it to your husband; nothing really happened anyway.

One day in the break room, he tells you how good you look. Then he invites you to lunch. He hasn't done anything inappropriate—not *really*—and you're enjoying the attention.

One weekend, when your husband is out of town, your coworker asks if he can drop some paperwork off to you on his way somewhere else. He comes by, and you get to chatting. It becomes more casual, more personal, and he suddenly confesses he has feelings for you. You tell him you feel the same way, but your marriage is much too important to you to do anything about it. You could never be unfaithful.

He leaves. You know you've stood the test, but you can't stop thinking of him and how good he makes you feel.

Those thoughts become an escape from the stress of marriage and the pressures of motherhood. You start texting back and forth with him, and the texts become more and more flirtatious. You tell yourself it's harmless. You've set the boundary, so where's the harm?

There are moments of conviction when you tell yourself this isn't healthy. You're risking your marriage, your family, and your future. But by now, you've become so tangled up in it that you can't seem to break free. You're hopelessly entangled.

Everyone is shocked when the affair inevitably is exposed. Two marriages end in divorce.

It's not that you decided to give up on your marriage. It's not that you consciously set out to quit on your husband and find someone else. But at some point, you were caught in the web, and by the time you realized it, you were too far gone.

Here's another web. As a teenager, you looked through a *Victoria's Secret* catalog that came in the mail. You couldn't get those images out of your mind. And then one day, on the internet, you discovered an endless collection of pictures like that. A few more clicks and, with a jolt, what you're looking at is much more explicit.

You secretly start spending hours on your device surfing the internet, searching for more images to consume.

You tell yourself you're not hurting anybody. You haven't really done anything wrong. It's not real; it's fantasy, enclosed in the confines of your imagination. What you've forgotten is the power of that imagination over you. In reality, you're entangled. You began by consuming images; now they consume you.

You get married—surely this will break the spell. You'll come loose from the web and walk into the sunset with the love of your life. For a while, things get a little easier, and you never share your secret struggle. It's past history.

Then one night, after it keeps coming to mind, you get on your device and log on to that familiar website. Immediately you're tangled up again. You never decided to quit on the intimacy of your marriage. You never consciously gave up on enjoying spiritual oneness with your wife. But something's wrong.

The years come and go, and the gap between the two of you widens. You don't pursue her, and pornography has turned you into a combination of a man simultaneously too harsh and too passive. Her heart has hardened, but you're too tangled up to notice. You are devastated when you find texts between her and her coworker. They're having an affair.

In your rage you say, "How could she do this to me?" But deep down you know the story is much more tangled than that.

Oh, You Mean *That* Sin

Hebrews 12 tells us to throw off the weight that hinders and the sin that so easily entangles.

We've talked about some commonly carried weights that slow us down and wear us out—but what is the sin that so easily entangles? The writer seems to be speaking of a specific sin. He doesn't speak of "sins" in the generic sense. So, what is that one sin that easily gets us tangled up?

I suppose a case could be made that whatever sin you picture as you read that verse is the sin that easily entangles you. And maybe that's the point. He's speaking of a singular and specific sin, and maybe the intention is for his readers to fill in the blank. What is the struggle that keeps tripping you up?

Maybe it's things. A friend of yours gets a new TV, wardrobe, car, or house, and you keep finding yourself dissatisfied and discontent with your own stuff.

Maybe it's retribution. Someone treated you wrongfully, and you had hoped for justice. Fair is fair. But it never came, and because you've stewed about it for so long, your desire for justice has turned into simple hate and loathing.

Maybe it's control. You feel invisible and ignored at your job or at home. So to break through that wall of disregard, you start falling into the trap of raging and yelling.

Maybe it's worth. You want to be affirmed for who you are, but to expedite that, you begin to conform and change who you are so you can get that affirmation you're wanting from others.

Maybe it's pleasure. You don't just pursue it—you worship it. It's where you look for comfort and hope. It's become the driver for your life.

Notice anything about those? They all start with something good and noble. You see, behind the snags and entanglement is something attractive, and that attraction calls out, deep down, to who we are. The issue comes when we abandon the place God has for those things and become enmeshed in an unhealthy attitude toward them.

Over the years, I've become friends with a good man who has battled a gambling addiction. In the beginning, he saw it as a harmless distraction, no different than blowing twenty bucks on a dinner; he'd drop that same amount on a poker game from time to time. Then some buddies invited him to go to Vegas, and the stakes got a little higher.

By the time the trip ended, he was down over seven thousand dollars. He'd maxed out his credit card and emptied his checking account. He couldn't tell his wife what happened, so he started telling one lie after another to try to explain their sudden financial stress. He made the classic mistake: he decided the way out of his problem was to double down on his problem. More gambling would get him out of the gambling web.

He took what they had in savings and started betting on the horses where I live in Kentucky. Three years later, he's maxed out thirteen credit cards; his gambling debts are in six figures. He's been fired for suspected embezzlement. His wife has moved out and is living with her parents. Deeper into the center of the web, farther from freedom.

But do you know what he said to me the last time we talked? "My luck is going to change, I can feel it." That's entangled.

Bloody Struggle

After we are told to throw off the sin that so easily entangles, what next? In Hebrews 12:4, the writer raises the stakes and tells us how seriously we should regard sin: "In your struggle against sin, you have not yet resisted to the point of your shedding blood."

To our modern ears, this sounds a little like a coach who sends his player back onto the field: "Get back out there! You're not even bleeding!" The idea in verse 4 is to put away these entanglements and keep running, because you haven't experienced *serious* resistance yet.

Maybe you've read *The Voyage of the Dawn Treader* by C. S. Lewis or saw the movie. It's an installment to the Chronicles of Narnia series. In the story, we meet Eustace, who's a truly annoying character to everyone around him, a spoiled kid. He is tricked and turned into a dragon.

It might sound pretty cool, but Eustace isn't pleased at all. He longs to be restored to his old human self. He gets his wish, but he's required to endure a painful transformation from dragon back to boy. You can feel Eustace's pain as you read about his anguish, dragon scale after dragon scale falling away from him. It's the author's way of helping us think about how difficult it is to throw off the monstrous entanglements we find ourselves in. Don't think this is going to be easy—but as the writer of Hebrews says, it could be a lot worse.

Apathetic and I Don't Care

Another problem: the more tangled up in sin you become, the less you seem to notice or care. Sin hardens your heart and makes you indifferent to the damage you may be doing to yourself. It also makes you oblivious to others who have become tangled up in your sin.

We feel no sense of urgency about it. We'll turn to God at some point; we're just waiting for a convenient time. But the problem is that a side effect of sin is a creeping indifference to sin. More and more, the sin seems like less and less.

Author Philip Yancey went out for a cup of coffee with a friend who admitted he was thinking of leaving his wife after fifteen years of marriage. He had fallen for someone younger and prettier. Yancey's friend was a Christian man with three kids. He asked, "Do you think God can forgive something as awful as what I'm about to do?"

In other words, he was asking, "Doesn't God have to give me another chance? Isn't God contractually obligated to forgive me and somehow work this out for my good down the road?"

The French philosopher Voltaire is credited with putting it this way: "God will always forgive—that's his job." A nice racket, if it really worked that way.

Yancey sat across the table from his friend for quite a while before answering the question. Here's what he finally said: "Can God forgive you? Of course. You know the Bible. The problem is the distance you'll place yourself from God—sin does that. It kills our closeness to him. Now you think of forgiveness, but will you want it then? Will you still care? God forgives. He doesn't change. The problem is that we do."[1]

Sin, over time, turns you into the proud type who rolls your eyes at the need for forgiveness. What you've done becomes the new normal. This is how sin gets us to give up on God. It doesn't happen all at once; it's a slow fade. An invisible web that becomes thicker toward the middle.

In Psalm 32, David speaks about the effect that his sin had on him. He got all tangled up with sin when he had an affair with Bathsheba. For a while he refused to deal with it, and ultimately it wore him down. David writes, "When I kept silent, my bones wasted away through my groaning all day long. For day and night your hand was heavy on me; my strength was sapped as in the heat of summer" (vv. 3–4).

When you're caught in a web, you go through all your resources of energy quickly, and you tire. Maybe you're experiencing that right now. A sticky strand of guilt pulls at you here. A silken filament of shame wraps around you there. You try to untangle yourself with denial and justification and rationalization—but nothing works.

Finally, as you run out of steam, you tell yourself there are worse things than being stuck in this web. Maybe this isn't so bad. You could make your home here. And you just kind of shrug, having been entangled in the stickiest strand of all: apathy.

Cutting Free from the Web of Shame

Sin is known for its many side effects, but two are prominent: guilt and shame. Guilt reminds us what we've done; shame tries to convince us what we've done is who we are.

The guilt of David's sin weighed him down, because guilt is an anchor to the past. And ships don't sail when the anchor is down. Try to move all you want, but that anchor holds. Eventually you'll blow the engine or run out of gas.

Guilt keeps you from moving, but shame tells you this is your destiny; you were meant to be stuck here. What you did last week is the story of your life; the book is written. It creates a full link between your failure and your identity. Self-condemnation is powerful, and it always points to the conclusion that we should give up.

Maybe something good happens. You feel a little momentum, and hope springs up that you might move forward in a brand-new direction. The ship moves, the chain plays out— and the anchor jerks you back. A little voice says, *Where did you think you were going?* Shame always comes to the surface.

Guilt and shame are difficult to overcome. I regularly visit local prisons and speak to the inmates. Often, when an inmate gets released, he comes to visit me at church. I've found that prisoners go through a cycle of elation to be free, followed by discouragement. That felony record follows them like an invisible chain. They wonder if they're truly free at all. Every time they apply for a new job, they have to check that tiny box with the huge consequences: *felon*. It's like going into an interview with your prison ID stamped on your cheek.

But this feeling doesn't require a prison record. At the end of the day, sometimes we climb into bed, turn out the lights, and think about all the should've dones. *I should've done this. I should've done that.*

In our minds, we begin to replay the highlights—or, more likely, the lowlights. *This is where I screwed up. This is where I couldn't keep my big mouth shut. This is where I missed my opportunity.*

It's mental quicksand. We put in a toe, then a foot, and pretty soon the emotions begin to suck us under. The embarrassment, then the guilt and shame. We reach for a vine, like Tarzan does in the movies—anything to keep us from going down. But it pulls relentlessly.

Maybe every night is a trip to the quicksand pit, and when we wake up the next day we're not refreshed, just mentally and emotionally exhausted, and even more sure that this is all we'll ever be: the sum total of a failed past.

The Wall of Sin

Sin separates us from God, then blames God for the separation. It builds the wall that cuts us off, then blames God for that wall.

One day, I got a text message from my neighbor saying that our dog had gotten out of our yard, come over to his house, and gotten one of his chickens.* There were feathers all over his driveway where the desperate battle had taken place.

My neighbor was letting me know that my dog had killed his chicken. I decided there were a few ways I could respond to this news:

1. I could ignore the texts and try to avoid him as long as possible. It would be awkward and inconvenient, but facing the guy would be even *more* awkward and inconvenient. This would probably mean the end of our friendship, but that's the price of avoiding sticky situations.

* Given the context I could guess what "gotten" meant.

2. I could pretend everything was okay and that nothing had happened. Next time I saw him, I could pretend nothing needed to be addressed. Except this friend is really good at repairing broken things around my house—when my annoying brother-in-law isn't available. If I ignored what happened, I wouldn't be able to ask him for help anymore.

3. I could blame him for it. He should have protected the chickens better. Hey, that's what dogs do. Everyone knows it's a dog-eat-chicken world out there.

These are some of the ways we tend to deal with sin: avoid God, those we've hurt, and the places involved; pretend it's all good and just push on; or put it all off on the other guy, because at all costs, we can't hit an issue head-on and admit we goofed up. Who does that?

I decided the way to deal with my neighbor was to try an Old Testament approach—offer him a penance, a gift of reconciliation. My wife was at the grocery store at the time all of this happened. I called to let her know that *her* dog had killed our neighbor's chicken and asked her to pick me up something from the peace offering aisle. Later that night, I took it over to him and apologized. You know what he received? A barbecue rotisserie chicken and a chocolate cake. Let the penitence fit the crime, I always say.

Hebrews explains to us that once there was a religious system God set up for helping us to deal with sin. It involved sacrifice, for example. But the system, like all systems, was misunderstood and abused.

Hebrews 10:1–4 teaches about why that system fell short and points out something interesting. Not only were these people having a hard time letting go of the old habits of religion but they were getting the whole thing backward anyway. Sacrifices were never intended to make people clean in any genuine way; these gifts were living reminders of the sin that was so inevitable in everyone's life. But somewhere along the way people began to think the sacrifices really made things right again: sin removed, case closed. We have a tendency to literalize.

If this were really the case, the writer asks, "Would they not have stopped being offered? For the worshipers would have been cleansed once for all, and would no longer have felt guilty for their sins" (Heb. 10:2).

Instead, the sin-and-sacrifice cycle just went on and on, part of life, nothing to see here. The readers of Hebrews needed to understand how sin really worked if they were going to avoid being entangled in it. Jesus did what the law could not: he gave himself as an offering on our behalf to make things right with God—one sacrifice for all time to break the cycle.

Therefore, concludes the writer, "Let us draw near to God with a sincere heart and with the full assurance that faith brings, having our hearts sprinkled to cleanse us from a guilty conscience and having our bodies washed with pure water" (v. 22).

As we've seen, we "come boldly" into the presence of Christ. Let him scrub away the guilt. Let the shame be rinsed once and for all. Make it good and thorough. When he washes us, we stay clean. No more cycles. No more anchors to the past. No more domination by regret and remorse. Jesus can take on every bit of it. He can wash it clean. He can free us up to start running the race as we should.

The Great Untangler

Jesus untangles us as only he can do. But how does it work? Leave it to Paul to get deep into the details of the process. He says that Jesus has shown us once and for all what it means to be clean, perfect, and righteous in a way we can never be. "For all have sinned and fall short of the glory of God, and all are justified freely by his grace through the redemption that came by Christ Jesus" (Rom. 3:23–24).

We say "nobody's perfect," but it's worse than that: nobody's even close. We're actually all disqualified at birth. The human race fails *en masse*—every single one of us earning judgment and punishment. We're fallen. We can't live a sinless moment.

But there's incredible news. News that sounds too good to be true—but it *is* true. None of our failures have to be counted. All of them can be forgiven, and the punishment we should receive can be assigned, all at once, to what Jesus endured in a crucifixion he never earned. He will trade his perfection, his righteousness for our shame, straight up.

Let's talk about the word *righteousness*. It's a nice church word, isn't it? Just think of it in a modern context as "proof of worth" or "proof of value."

My second oldest daughter is currently applying to colleges. When she fills out an application, she is being asked to provide proof of her worthiness. They don't let in just anybody. She has to list her grades, her test scores, and whatever experiences or accomplishments might make the case that she's worthy of being accepted.

If you've put together a résumé or filled out a credit application recently, then you've done the same thing. You've had to show you're "righteous" enough to be accepted, to be hired, to get the loan.

Both Romans and Hebrews point out that under the law, no one is righteous enough. No one has the grades or a good enough credit score, so you might as well give up. Under the law, your application has been denied, and your résumé has been rejected.

But now there's a righteousness apart from the law, meaning you don't have to come up with impossible credentials, showing you've never sinned, never screwed up, never fallen short. Jesus lived that life for you. He says, "Here's how it's done," then takes those credentials and places them in your hands. "When they get to your case, just show them this," he says.

We only need the faith to let Christ represent us. If we do, we're judged worthy; we're good to go.

"All are justified freely by his grace through the redemption that came by Christ Jesus" (v. 24). Can you imagine what that means? We are "justified freely." You might hear that and assume that *justified* is just a synonym for *forgiven*. It begins there, but it goes a lot further than that. We're not only forgiven for our failures but credited for the righteousness of Jesus. It's like being told that not only did you make the team but you have all the stats and honors of the greatest player ever.

The doctrinal term for this is *imputed righteousness. Impute*, a word we don't use much these days, means "to credit." Jesus has a perfect credit score in righteousness, and it's imputed to us.

Some people hear that and their eyebrows go up a little. "That doesn't seem very fair. People should get what they deserve, right? I can't get a 100 on a test at school, take my paper to the teacher, and say, 'Count this for the dummy in the third row.' A bank won't consider the credit rating of the guy down the street before giving me a loan." True, but verse 25 explains how God pulls this off: "God presented Christ as a sacrifice of atonement, through the shedding of his blood—to be received by faith." *Atonement*, of course, is at-one-ment. The sacrifice makes us at-one, or at peace, with God.

Paul explains so much of this in his letter to the Romans. God didn't ignore our sin, simply looking the other way and saying, "No big deal." That's where unfairness would have come in. The debt was the largest possible—*all* the sin of the whole world. So God paid that debt with the ultimate sacrifice—*all* the perfection and purity of the Son of God.

No, this wasn't simply a "look the other way" thing. It involved incredible pain and sacrificial love. Our sin was imputed to the perfect one, while his righteousness was imputed to the worst sinners imaginable—if we accept the gift. As Paul puts it through *The Message* paraphrase: "How? you ask. In Christ. God put the wrong on him who never did anything wrong, so we could be put right with God" (2 Cor. 5:21).

Sometimes we hear the gospel explained with the example of a courtroom. We stand before God and he pulls out our record—all the things we've done wrong. We start to panic, because it's a thick document, thousands of pages long. But, as this particular story goes, our faith in Christ renders those pages blank. The moment we said yes to Jesus, it was all stricken from the record. Nothing we could say or do could be held against us.

That's a great metaphor, but through his Son, God has done so much more than that. The pages aren't blank at all—they're filled with everything wonderful about Jesus. The book has been fully rewritten with a perfect and powerful record. Too often this is missed. We imagine a stern God in the seat of judgment, listening to the advocacy of Jesus, then looking at us with a scowl and allowing us to slip into heaven, kind of on a legal technicality. By the skin of our teeth.

That's not what it means to be heirs of Christ. Instead, it's more like God looks into our eyes and sees his own Son in us. He smiles. He throws his arms around us and says again how much he loves us. And he says, "We have so much work to do in this world. Let's get to it!"

The operative element in the story is faith. The power is all in Christ, but faith is the button that activates it. Do you have that faith? Do you believe Jesus is better than your sin and can take that entire load off your back?

The Sin of Unbelief

We've noticed that the writer of Hebrews talks about *the* sin that so easily entangles—not Sin, but a particular sin. What is it?

We've also said that the answer might be a little different for each of us, but I've come to believe there's an in-general answer too: *unbelief*. Every other sin is rooted in unbelief because, of course, it's the opposite of faith. If faith is the button that activates every wonderful thing that can happen in our lives, unbelief is the refusal to push it.

Hebrews 11:1 defines faith this way: "Now faith is confidence in what we hope for and assurance about what we do not see." If so, then unbelief is an uncertainty in what God has said and a skepticism about what we do not see.

Faith has confidence that God is trustworthy; unbelief doubts his intentions and integrity.

Faith believes God weeps with us; unbelief thinks God is ambivalent and doesn't care about our hurts.

Faith trusts God for a spouse; unbelief takes matters into our own hands.

Faith honors God with our money; unbelief decides we need to take care of ourselves.

Faith believes God cares for every hair on our head; unbelief decides he doesn't want to know us.

Faith trusts that righteousness is given to us through Jesus; unbelief doubts that we can be made right.

Faith enables us to repent of our sin, knowing we can be forgiven; unbelief convinces us we are too far gone.

If you imagine a weightlifter straining to lift a barbell loaded with heavy weights, you might imagine stress on one side of the bar and anxiety on the other. Those are the primary weights that are so heavy—but unbelief is the bar they're attached to. We feel stress and anxiety because of our unbelief in God's ability to take care of us.

Do I really believe God is my refuge and strength and an ever-present help in trouble? (Ps. 46:1)

Do I really believe that in all things, God works for the good of those who love him? (Rom. 8:28)

Do I really believe that nothing can separate me from the love of God? (Rom. 8:39)

Do I really believe that God's mercies are infinite and new every morning? (Lam. 3:22–23)

These are things we say. They need to be things we believe or we'll stagger under the weight of our unbelief.

Maybe you struggle with greed because you don't believe that Jesus satisfies. Maybe you struggle with lust because you don't believe what God teaches about sexuality. Maybe you struggle with selfishness because you don't believe it's better to give than to receive.

Maybe you struggle with discouragement because you don't believe that God is at work. Maybe you struggle with anger because you don't really believe in God's grace. Maybe you struggle with bitterness because you don't believe that God is just. Maybe you struggle with control because you don't believe God can be trusted. Maybe you struggle with fear because you don't believe in God's sovereignty. Maybe you struggle with anxiety because you don't believe God really cares.

Maybe you struggle with guilt because you don't really believe God can forgive you. Maybe you struggle with shame because you don't really believe God has made you new. Maybe you struggle with wanting to give up because you don't really believe you can do all things through Christ who gives you strength.

As a pastor I often talk with couples who are ready to give up on their marriage. The relationship has become so tangled up by sin it seems impossible to move forward. Often they have already been to counseling and tried to work through their issues. Whenever I talk to one of these couples who are ready to quit, I ask them to do something before they throw in the towel. I ask them to meet with a friend of mine named Cassie Soete. I've asked her to share her story with you.

When I said "I do" to George, on September 7, 1964, I thought it would be a Cinderella story. We were crazy about each other and thought that's how it would always be. We were cruising through life. We were blessed with six beautiful children—four little girls, very close in age, then, after a nine-year gap, we had our surprise son, Jeff, and another daughter two years later.

We had a pretty normal marriage of mostly successful "ups," but over the years, our marriage took a backseat as I focused all my time on the kids and George stayed busy building his career.

It was on our twentieth anniversary that George told me he was leaving me to marry a close friend of ours.

It was chaos. I actually thought I was going to die. What would I do? How could I raise six kids on my own?

I told him if he was going to leave, he'd have to tell the children. He did, and they were sobbing. It felt as if time stood still in that horrible moment. Out of this heartache, I fell in complete surrender to Jesus, constantly on my knees, praying with every breath. I began to know, love, and serve God in a way I never had before, and, as I prayed, I felt this nudging from God not to give up on my marriage.

This began a four-and-a-half-year journey with two sets of divorce papers.

George came in and out of our lives eight different times over these years. Each time, we thought he'd be home to stay, but each time he would leave again. Each time he came and left, my friends and some of my family members became increasingly adamant that I should give up on our marriage and be done with George once and for all.

But the stronger I got in my faith, the more George saw the change in me over those years. I was no longer dependent on him to make me happy or somehow complete me. Jesus was doing that. One night, in his apartment, George told me he wanted the peace that I had. That night he surrendered his life to Christ and came back home to stay in 1988. As we were healing together, he promised me, "You'll live to see the day that you forgive me. You'll live to see the day that you trust me again, and you'll live to see the day that you know I love you more than anything on the face of this earth, short of Jesus Christ."

And I did.

We spent our lives together, helping others in troubled marriages through a ministry we helped to form called the Marriage Mentoring Ministry. George went to be with Jesus on April 7, 2015, and the night before he died, he told me how very much he loved me, and how thankful he was that I never once "quit" on him. He had such a redeeming life, and we had such an unbelievable marriage. Nearly two thousand people from our years of ministry together came to pay their respects at his funeral visitation.

Maybe your marriage seems beyond repair. Maybe there are some people telling you that you should give up and be done. Maybe that seems like the only option. I'm here to tell you that God can still redeem and restore what is broken. Don't give up!

When our guilt turns into shame, then our sin becomes our identity. When we start to identify ourselves by our sin, then it can feel like a permanently attached weight from which we will never be free. When we believe that what we have done is who we are, then we will lose heart. It will feel impossible to move forward under the weight of our shame and guilt, and eventually we will give up.

Realize today that your identity isn't based in what you've done or what you haven't done. It's based in what Jesus has done for you. God looks upon you and sees Christ. He sees purity, righteousness, infinite possibility.

Once there were terrible words to describe who you were: cheater, dropout, fired employee, inattentive parent, squanderer of ambitions. Those words are empty in your case now; void, N/A. You are a new creation in Christ. You are forgiven. You are righteous. You are beloved. You are a full heir to the kingdom of God.

Next time you feel caught in the web, realize you don't need to be there. Jesus, the great untangler, came to set you free. Don't give up. He has freed you from the weight of sin and shame.

The question is, *Do you believe it?*

Run Your Race

Marla Runyon arrived in Sydney, Australia, in the year 2000. She had been legally blind for twenty-two years. When she looked at the world, she saw no colors, no clear definition—just what she described as a "fuzzy blob," all in black and white. She had a degenerative retina condition known as Stargardt's Disease.

Not that any of that stopped her from running in the Summer Olympic Games in Sydney. She qualified for the finals in the 1,500-meter race, though she finished just behind the medal winners.

It was actually her second Olympics. In Atlanta, in 1996, she had originally gone to the trials for the seven-event heptathlon. She finished no better than tenth, and was close to retiring from track and field in discouragement. Except that somebody noticed she won the 800-meter run, the final event, and set an American record doing it.

She was invited to try out as an 800 meter runner. She hired a new coach and became a dedicated middle-distance runner—despite the fact she was running blind. And she won race after race, eventually moving to greater distances and winning gold at the 1999 Pan-American Games in Winnipeg.

Marla said that when she ran, she simply focused on the "blob" of bodies ahead of her and tried to get in front of it. That final turn, she said, was the hardest. She could rarely make out anything and wasn't even certain whether she was on the final stretch. She learned to listen to the announcer and the crowd, she set her course for the finish line—and she kept on running.

As we've seen, Hebrews 12 sees life as not only a race but a race with obstacles and entanglements. Like Marla, we become discouraged when we can't see the course ahead too clearly—there are times when the future is no better than a fuzzy blob. Other times we can't tell whether we're in the homestretch or if the course is going to take yet another turn. The main thing is to keep running.

In preparing to write this book, I paged through the Bible's references to running and was surprised by how much of this activity happens throughout the Scriptures. We're familiar with the footraces mentioned in Hebrews and in some of Paul's letters. It was a Greek thing. The writers found races to be the perfect metaphor, because they're all about getting from here to there swiftly. They demand conditioning and high exertion. And, of course, an award (described as a crown) awaits those who run the race well.

But even in the Old Testament, before the Greeks and their racing craze, we notice David saying the sun is "like a champion rejoicing to run his course" (Ps. 19:5). We're told in 1 Samuel that kings showed off their power by having fleet soldiers who ran ahead with the horsemen. And an often cynical Solomon, in Ecclesiastes, comments that the race isn't always won by the fastest runner.

Hold that thought.

I really love the fact that as we come to the resurrection accounts in the Gospels, suddenly everybody's running everywhere.

All four Gospels mention people running at the news of the empty tomb. Mary runs to tell the disciples. Peter and John have a memorable footrace to the tomb the moment they're told the news. (John wants us to know he beat his opponent to the finish line, but it's Peter, with his typical lack of restraint, who barges right into the tomb itself.)

This made me realize that running isn't strictly competitive; it isn't just to get from Point A to Point B. Racing is *emotional*—a high-intensity activity for high-intensity moments.

It's motivated by fear (Mark 16:8), sheer exhilaration (Matt. 28:8), or incredible curiosity (John 20:2–4). What Jesus did brought about strong emotions that often surfaced in running.

Those are sprints; life is a marathon. And about that—when we set out to go the distance, it's not going to be easy. Eventually the emotion wears off. Soon the pain sets in. At some point the challenge of running your race comes down to whether you will give up or keep going.

As Ecclesiastes reminds us, speed alone is no guarantee. The race isn't always to the swift or the battle to the strong. Sometimes it goes to those who simply refuse to give up. Occasionally, like Marla, you may find yourself running blind. That's when you lean forward and push yourself, legs churning in sheer faith, with your eyes on the prize.

Consider this section a dry run for the race that lies ahead—the course laid out between where you are now and the incredible destiny God has in mind for you. Expect obstacles. Look for setbacks. Just remember, this is the race that has been marked out for you. Marla found out she was designed for middle distance, and she ran straight into the history books. What does God have in mind for you?

8

Obstacle Course

One day my wife informed me she'd signed us up for a four-mile run. This was part of her master plan to get us back in shape after the holidays. I told her sure, I was up for it—though I'm not certain she was actually asking my permission. She was conveying information, not offering an invitation.

About a month later, she was checking in on how I was preparing for the run. But I noticed something; she wasn't talking about a "run" anymore. Somehow it had become an "obstacle course." When I asked about the change in terminology, she innocently said, "Oh, didn't I mention the twenty-five obstacles during the four-mile run?"

"What kind of obstacles?" I asked, my Spidey-sense tingling.

"Doesn't matter," she dodged, kissing me on the cheek. "You're man enough for *any* obstacles."

She had a point. How was I supposed to argue with that? Thus she neatly maneuvered me toward an experience I would never have knowingly agreed to. See, I pictured a nice run with little stops along the way where I'd do a dozen push-ups or pull-ups, then run some more.

Instead, I found myself throwing my body into patches of mud and army crawling under barbed wire that scratched my back, as if we were preparing for the beaches of Okinawa. Then I'd unpucker myself from the mud, run another quarter mile, and hit the monkey bars. That sounds like fun, I know. Hey, monkey bars! But these were *twenty yards* of monkey bars that real monkeys would have looked at once and said, "Nope."

I ignored the scratches on my back, the dripping mud on my belly, and the searing pain in my forearms as I navigated the bars, wondering whether I should just let go and plunge into the four feet of mud below me.

After running another quarter mile, I was carrying a tractor tire on my shoulders while trying to hike up a mud-slick hill. Mud was kind of the theme of everything and it was everywhere. I had mud in places I didn't know I had places.

After completing half the course, I called it a day. Well, that's not really what happened. Basically I cheated. I sort of kept running or limping past the obstacles. I figured that since I was a big mud-blob by this time, no one could ID me anyway.

I was exhausted. I was humbled. I'd been ready for a four-mile run in the sunshine. It was the obstacles that took me down.

Hebrews 12 invites us to "run with perseverance the race marked out for us" (v. 1). Easier said than done—I know that now.

This word *race*, in the Greek, is *agon*. It's where we get our word *agony*. The word indicates that the race marked out for us is no "fun run." It's difficult and demanding, a challenging race. This isn't a jog on the beach; it's running until your sides hurt and your lungs burn and your muscles begin to cramp. But you don't give up; you keep running.

The Bible doesn't tell us to mark out our race just the way we like it and run—it's been marked out for us, so we don't choose its difficulty level, nor do we receive a map of the obstacles that lie ahead. If it were up to us, we'd run along a tropical beach and downhill all the way. Water stations would wait all along the route, and there would be an awesome song mix pumping out of the speakers.*

Some Christians expect life to be a fun run simply because they've signed up with Jesus. The whole *point* of signing up for some of us was to avoid obstacles. Regular life has too many of them. Yet they are part of the plan. One way we know we're running the race marked out for us is the presence of regular, unexpected challenges.

As you study through Scripture, you'll find that those who faithfully ran the race God marked out for them had to deal with one obstacle after another. The faith heroes faced significant and surprising obstacles. That's the theme of the entire chapter that precedes Hebrews 12:1.

Nehemiah ran that kind of race. His story comes at a troubling, humbling time for the people of Israel. They've been exiles in a foreign land, humiliated and dragged off into bondage. Nehemiah's book is essentially a 2,500-year-old prayer journal.

In 587 BC, the Babylonians conquered the Israelites and hauled away everyone who could serve them. Then the Persian

* Also: no mud.

Empire rose up and conquered the Babylonians. This is the time when we catch up with Nehemiah, an Israelite in a far-away land.

He lives in the capital city of Persia, where he works in a prominent position as a cupbearer to the king. Among other duties, he tastes the wine to make sure it hasn't been poisoned. Nehemiah is an Israelite who has probably never seen his homeland, never set foot in Jerusalem. Israel was one thousand miles away, and most of its people hadn't been back for one hundred and forty years.

Nehemiah heard that his home city of Jerusalem was in ruins, its walls destroyed and its gates burned down. In Nehemiah 1:4, he tells us how he responds when he hears the condition of the Holy City: "I sat down and wept. For some days I mourned and fasted and prayed before the God of heaven."

He is emotionally devastated to hear that his home has been laid waste. Jerusalem, so bright and beautiful in his imagination, was utterly fallen. After days of prayer and fasting, he emerges with the firm assurance he has to do something. God laid it on his heart to get moving.

He has a comfortable life in the inner circle of the palace, but he is willing to give that up. It was time to enter the race. But it was also time to discover many of the basic obstacles we all face.

The Obstacle of Indifference

Indifference is the mother of all obstacles, because it can keep us from even running. Nehemiah could have said, "Well, Jerusalem is a thousand miles away, and I've never been there.

What does it have to do with my life? Besides, nobody else is doing anything."

Psychologists talk about the "bystander effect." This is the phenomenon that takes place when someone watches something bad occurring nearby—an obvious call to action—but the person doesn't do anything. The "bystander effect" has become a more significant problem as more and more people seem more concerned with filming an event on their phones than intervening.

In Kansas City, a young lady was assaulted in the middle of the day in a parking lot. Ten people witnessed it. Two people recorded it on their phones. Nobody lifted a hand to help—or even to call the police. The bystander effect would suggest that those people aren't evil or wicked; they just saw themselves as spectators rather than responders. One theory is that in a crowd, we believe someone else will do something. Most of us don't see ourselves as step-forward, take-charge types.

Do you remember that old cartoon character Popeye? I used to love him when I was a kid. The villain, Brutus, would sometimes give Popeye's girlfriend, Olive Oyl, a hard time. There's even a character named Wimpy. He's an eater, not a fighter. Interestingly, Popeye always puts up with a lot of bad stuff before he takes action. Finally he says those same words he always says: "That's all I can stand, and I can't stand no more!" Then he becomes a fighting machine, generally with a spinach boost of some kind.

If I see a wrong that needs righting, how long before I "can't stand no more"? Maybe it's just that "I yam what I yam, and that's all that I yam." Maybe I'm too wimpy. Maybe there just isn't enough spinach in the world.

We need to overcome our apathy. This is a huge obstacle to being God's people today. We give up before we've done anything. But how do we start caring?

Jerusalem had been burned and broken for so long. When a situation has been bad for such a long time, there's a natural tendency to lose interest. It's just the way things have always been, and it's the way things will always be. We shrug. Our tolerance to the brokenness has become high, and the tendency is to think, *It's too late.*

But what if, instead of saying it's too late, we started saying, "That's all I can stand, and I can't stand no more"?

Nehemiah has reached that point. He knows it's time to get on the track and start running. But what can he do?

Another explanation of the bystander effect is the belief that nothing can be done. A person thinks, *I'm not qualified. I'm too old. I'm too young. I'm not smart enough. I don't have the resources.*

No one would blame Nehemiah for thinking that. He lives a thousand miles away. He works directly for a king who would be threatened if the walls of Jerusalem were rebuilt and the city reestablished. He has no reason to see a revived Israel. The king's official foreign policy concerning Jerusalem is that it's not to be touched.

Thus anyone else in Nehemiah's sandals would take one look at the situation and say, "Nothing can be done."

The Obstacle of Insufficiency

Nehemiah looks at the race marked out for him and realizes he's in no way equipped to deal with the known obstacles, not to mention the countless unknown ones.

Think about the size of the challenge, the distance of it, the danger of it.

But he has a powerful conviction. He's anything but apathetic. He's not sure what he can do, but he believes he must act.

One of the ways you know you're running the race that God has marked out for you is that you realize you're insufficient and unqualified for what you're facing. There's no way to run it without God's power and provision. If you try to do it out of your own strength, you'll quickly grow weak. If you try to do it out of your own confidence, you will be humbled. What you're going to do requires dependence on God and the power of the Holy Spirit.

Nehemiah knows full well that on paper there is no way for him to run this race. He doesn't have what it takes. He doesn't have the position, the power, or the resources. That's not being negative or fatalistic. It's simple truth.

So how does he overcome the obstacle of insufficiency? He begins to pray. There doesn't seem to be much more he can do in his position—but there's nothing more powerful. By the time we get to chapter 2, four months have passed. He prays and keeps praying, but nothing seems to be happening.

Nehemiah understood prayer as the real work, not a quick activity at some designated time. Yet it requires patience. Nehemiah prays for four months and doesn't even feel as if he's out of the starting blocks. Nothing is happening—until one day, when he is bringing wine to the king, the king sees the anxiety in Nehemiah's face and asks him about it. And Nehemiah's whole story comes flooding out. He could take the safe route and say, "Oh, it's nothing." But he's counting on God to answer his prayers. Maybe this is his moment.

In Nehemiah 2:2–4, he explains that his face is sad because his ancestral city lies in ruins. You can feel the passion in him as you read his words to the king. And the king, apparently moved, asks, "What is it you want?"

God has opened the king's heart. Nehemiah asks for the royal blessing to go home and rebuild. It's a stunning request, yet the king gives him permission, timber, and armed guards—he completely buys in.

For four months, it has seemed for all the world that God wasn't listening. Yet Nehemiah has waited upon the Lord. He has been patient. And finally he hears those words: "What do you want?"

We move quickly forward in time, and Nehemiah is now in Jerusalem with his delegation, preparing for work. If I were him, I'd be thinking *I got through all the obstacles! I have wood for building and soldiers for protection. The wind is at my back now.*

It's never a good time to think that, because the course allows for all kinds of obstacles.

The Obstacle of Opposition

Nehemiah and his workers are into the project—they've started, but quickly they're facing opposition. A couple of local governing rulers don't want the walls of Jerusalem to be rebuilt. They're threatened by the progress being made, and they try to trip up Nehemiah as he runs the race.

We read in chapter 4 that a local leader named Sanballat begins to ridicule the Jews. He taunts them, saying they'll never succeed. Tobiah the Ammonite, his buddy, makes what he thinks is a terrific joke. If a fox climbed up on their wall, the wall would break down, he says. Your basic trolling.

Nehemiah has said yes to God, and that means saying yes to facing opposition. That's just how it works. Sometimes we say, "I ran into a problem. That means this isn't God's will." We get the idea that a smooth track proves God is on our side; bumps in the road are a heavenly thumbs-down. But what if it's just the opposite? Sometimes, when you face roadblocks, you know you must be doing the right thing.

Do you remember Newton's Third Law of Motion? It'll come back to you. "Every action has an equal and opposite reaction."

What's true in the physical realm tends to play out in the spiritual realm. For every spiritual action, there is an equal and opposite spiritual reaction. So when you set out to rebuild, you're taking action consistent with the character of God. He's a creator, a restorer, a rebuilder. But while your action aligns with his character, it opposes Satan, who is at his core a destroyer.

God creates; Satan destroys. And when you begin to be a part of rebuilding what Satan has destroyed, there will be opposition. Expect that your construction effort will be met with an equal and opposite attempt at destruction.

Nehemiah wasn't facing opposition because he was doing something wrong but because he was doing something right. That means opposition shouldn't discourage us but make us more determined. We attack, evil counterattacks, and that's when we should be ready to dig in and fight. If we think of opposition as an indication that we are not running the race God has marked out for us, then we'll give up and quit when things get difficult.

Consider these scenarios:

I'm constantly fighting with my spouse. Maybe I missed
    God's will and married the wrong person.
Our house still hasn't sold. Maybe God didn't want me to
    move to a different town and start a new job.
My kids keep fighting with me. I must be a horrible parent.
This degree is full of trials. Maybe I need to drop out.
My parents don't get me. They must not love me.
I keep praying for God to change this. He hasn't. I'm done.

Nehemiah is opposed by people who are insecure and
jealous. Seven times in Nehemiah, we find a consistent
cycle: the work advances, they get a little momentum, then
the opposition tries to stop them through criticism and
ridicule.

Maybe you're experiencing some of that in your rebuilding efforts. Your efforts are an indictment against them, so
they start to do their best to discourage you through criticism, ridicule, and gossip.

Did you ever have the annoying neighbor who has the perfectly manicured lawn? This is the kind of guy who has the
checkerboard pattern cut into his grass, and no one in the
neighborhood likes him. You don't want to be neighbors with
this guy, because his excellence is an indictment against your
mediocrity.

When you start to rebuild, people whom you'd expect to
be supportive and encouraging are sometimes critical and
discouraging. A spouse acts annoyed about your new spiritual commitment. A buddy gives you a hard time about quit-

ting drinking. You change some priorities and a neighbor writes you off.

Discouraging people make it difficult to endure. I want to challenge you to be an encourager in someone else's rebuilding efforts today. The right word from you at just the right time can make all the difference in someone's life.

As I worked on this chapter, I was in the midst of a tough week. On Thursday, I was way behind on a few things and feeling discouraged and tired. I got a text from my wife that said, "Praying for you right now—for energy, strength, and productiveness. Love you!"

That word of encouragement from the right person at the right time made all the difference. I caught a second wind and kept running.

In Hebrews 10, the writer challenges these believers to encourage each other as fellow runners:

> Let us consider how we may spur one another on toward love and good deeds, not giving up meeting together, as some are in the habit of doing, but encouraging one another. (vv. 24–25)

Stop for a moment and consider how you might spur on someone in your life who is struggling and discouraged. How can you notice their efforts? How can you appreciate their progress? Who's facing some opposition and needs to be spurred on? There's a strange thing that happens when you intentionally encourage others: you will be encouraged yourself.

When you run the race God has marked out, you can expect opposition. That was true for the Christians who were living the book of Hebrews. They'd made progress in their faith but now they were dealing with opposition and persecution.

If you're content to stay back with the pack and not push ahead, and if you're fine with the status quo—chances are you won't hear much. But as soon as you start running, as soon as you do something, there will be criticism. That's how the opposition begins: they criticize and ridicule. They make fun of your effort and try to discourage you with words. The barrage is relentless, and it can hurt.

People often react one of two ways to opposition. They either become discouraged or they become determined. Nehemiah becomes more determined, but soon the opposition moves from criticizing to threatening. They threaten to attack anyone who is rebuilding the wall.

Despite the opposition, the progress continues. The wall is rebuilt to half its height, and we're told the people work "with all their heart" (Neh. 4:6). In other words—first half, so far, so good.

That's the story of a lot of my little household projects. I do the first half with great energy. I stand back, admire my work, and congratulate myself. Then I make a sandwich. Then a couple of weeks later, I realize it's still half-done.

In the middle of dealing with the opposition, Nehemiah is faced with yet another obstacle.

The Obstacle of Slow Progress

The people start with strength and determination, but as they start rebuilding the wall, they realize how much there is to do. They grow tired, and there's so much rubble around them.

The people are ready to give up. We also have a lot of half-done projects:

My kids are too out of control.

My marriage is too broken.

My friend is too bitter.

My house is a lost cause.

I'm in too much debt to climb out.

Have you ever started cleaning and felt overwhelmed? We start off ready to build, but after a few days or weeks, we get discouraged. We thought it would be quicker than this. We thought people would be more receptive. And, like the laborers on the wall, we find our strength is giving out. We want to endure, but like the people found in Nehemiah 4:10, we begin to grow impatient.

At some point we think, *What's the point?*

Three days into your diet, you go to the state fair and order a Krispy Kreme double cheeseburger with chocolate covered bacon.*

A month ago, you committed to paying off your debt, and you started strong. But then you saw you had a little cash balance, and you grabbed your credit card and headed to the mall.

You go for a week of praying with your spouse, but then one night you get in a fight and lose your temper.

Too much work. Too much rubble. Maybe it's just time to give up. What are we supposed to do when the obstacles add up, we grow tired, and all we can see is uncleared rubble?

---

* Yep, we have those in Kentucky.

1. Embrace the obstacles.

As you read Nehemiah's story, it becomes clear that he faces the obstacles head-on. He doesn't back down or step away or pretend that something is easy when, in fact, it's extraordinarily difficult. Nehemiah actually goes off by himself and examines the condition of the walls. He pays attention to what he's up against and takes notes on the challenges he will have to face.

Too often we do the opposite: we resort to avoidance and denial. Instead of doing a deep dive into our financial situation, we say, "I can't face it," and close the books. We leave bills unopened and pretend everything is fine. If our marriage is struggling, we don't talk about it; we retreat to our corners and pretend there isn't a problem.

The path of least resistance is tempting. For me, when I was covered with mud and scratches, I started dodging the obstacles altogether.

Nehemiah does something else—he rallies the troops. He calls them all together and says, "You may have noticed that we're supposed to be building a wall, but instead we've hit a wall." He doesn't candy-coat it. He faces the problem head-on, calls it by its name, shows no fear of it. Denial is not an effective way of dealing with obstacles. It takes courage to be honest with ourselves and others about the state of the crisis.

Honest doesn't mean negative, of course. He doesn't vent all over everyone. He doesn't rant or blame. He states the situation, then expresses confidence in God for their continuing work. Then he says, "Let us start rebuilding" (2:18).

Take a moment and think about an area of your life that needs rebuilding. The rubble has kept you away. You've told yourself at some point you will address the mess, but you intentionally avoid it. Procrastination is often just a way of not giving up all at once. It takes courage to identify and honestly assess the situation. To embrace the obstacles.

2. Persevere in prayer.

We also observe that whenever Nehemiah faces an obstacle, he prays. In some ways, this is the theme of the book. From the time he hears about the devastation of the walls, he prays at every juncture. This book is a prayer journal, and that allows us to learn about how to pray when confronted with obstacles.

First, Nehemiah finds courage by reminding himself who God is. He prays about "the God of heaven, the great and awesome God" (1:5).

He doesn't ask for help by reminding God how deserving he is; he makes a humble request founded in God's character. He begins with praise.

When we start our prayer with worship, we're reminded of God's greatness. Things fall into perspective, and God shows us situations as they really are. We realize he is sovereign, and nothing in this world, even our problem, is bigger than he is. If he could speak the universe into existence, he's up to whatever challenge we're facing. The more we praise God, the more we enumerate his infinite, awesome qualities, the more clearly we see. The more boldly we trust. The more we feel our strength return.

Second, when Nehemiah prays, he finds courage by reminding himself what God has done for his people. Nehemiah then brings his people before God as part of his praise.

"They are your servants," he prays (v. 10). He revisits the history of God rescuing his people from Egyptian slavery.

Reviewing God's history in our life and the lives of others also gives us perspective. It reminds us that he is trustworthy and faithful, and our confidence and courage grow.

"God, I'm at my wits' end in this situation. I have nowhere to turn. But as I read your Word, as I see how you care for those who love you, I know you'll take care of me too. Will you guide me, Lord? Will you give me the strength to keep going?"

"God, I've lost my job, and I'm not sure how I'm going to provide some of my family's basic needs. But in Exodus 16, you dropped food down from heaven. In John 6, when your people were hungry, you took a little boy's lunch and multiplied it. Would you find a way to take care of us too?"

"God, there is no peace in my home. I'm constantly fighting with my spouse. My kids are always yelling at each other. But I've been reading Mark 4, about a huge storm raging and how you commanded it to be still. Would you calm the storm in our household?"

Prayer connects us to the wonderful truths about God. What he has done before, he can do again. Nehemiah finds confidence and courage in prayer by remembering who God is, what God has done, and lastly by remembering the promises God has made. In 1:8–9, he reviews how God dealt with Moses, and how God promised that if the people were obedient, God would bring them to the place he had chosen for them.

This is why it's so important that we steep our minds and hearts in God's Word. Our simple familiarity with Scripture will bring God's great works to mind as we cry out to him for help. He'll reach into our memory banks and bring psalms and praises and stories to mind.

Nehemiah prays and grows in confidence concerning a very simple but powerful truth, and he speaks this truth to the people: "Our God will fight for us!" (4:20). It's a ringing declaration, and it shows Nehemiah's mentality. How can you give up when you know that "our God will fight for us"?

When you see God as a warrior, and you know you're fighting for his causes, you have every right to feel strong and courageous.

3. Just keep building.

When it's time to run, just keep running. No matter what. In Nehemiah's case, he just keeps building. Yes, he says, "Our God will fight for us." But he gets ready to do his part in the fight.

Initially, he tells the people to pray and to post a guard. Then, when the threats become more serious, Nehemiah tells the people to defend their families, to fight, and to remember God's greatness. Meanwhile, he tells them, keep right on building!

We read something amazing next. People carried building materials in one hand and weapons in the other. Bricklayers armed themselves with swords as well as trowels. The building wasn't going to stop—no matter what. Imagine the picture this presented to the spies watching them.

Sometimes it seems right to stop and deal with obstacles. But if at all possible, we should continue to run the race, to do the work God set for us to do. Show you mean business.

Just keep building. Keep running. Keep doing what God has called you to do.

Huddle Up, Men

You may have noticed that, in this particular section of Nehemiah, he speaks directly to men. There's no reason men and women can't both benefit from these verses, but there's particularly good wisdom for men here.

God has called men to be builders and protectors. Running the race that he has marked out for us means carrying a trowel in one hand and a sword in the other. Candidly, I'm tired of hearing men make excuses for why they quit building or quit fighting. There are few things more annoying to me than hearing grown men whine about how hard the race is. I want to ask, "What did you expect? Did you think you could build a wall and no one would pay attention?"

Don't take this the wrong way, but why step onto a battlefield, then start crying when someone takes a shot at you? You don't hear a football player whining on the sideline because a mean person tried to tackle him.

The trowel is never put away. The fantasy of some men is to crawl into the man cave at home and be left alone because we went to work or did some other chore. We think we've earned a holiday from responsibility. Soon it becomes an excuse for almost never laying any bricks.

Men, can we just agree that we're going to put down the remote control and pick up the sword to fight for our marriage? That we're going to put down the PlayStation controller and pick up the trowel to build up our family?

Can we agree that we're going to put down the cell phone

when our wife walks in the room, and we're going to look her in the eye and honor her as a daughter of God?

Can we agree that we'll push pause on the big game and go kneel beside our kid's bed and pray?

Can we just agree that our families are about building, about fighting for what's right, about running without stopping to chill? Battlefields have no rest stops or nap times. The time is always now to do what needs doing, to defend the poor and the overlooked, the widows and orphans, the hurting and the helpless.

We need to serve God with a sense of urgency.

Talk to the Hand

Now the letters start coming—four of them. Nehemiah's enemies are writing him, calling out for him to stop that building right now and take a meeting. That's right. Their next tactic is the committee meeting. It's a sharp strategy because a committee meeting can kill almost anything.

Nehemiah receives the four letters and sends four replies. In chapter 6, we see that he basically tells them, "Why should I stop when I'm on a roll? Why should I come to your place?" If the trolls want to talk, they can stand under the ladder and have their say.

Nehemiah has a lot to teach us about endurance. First, just keep praying. Second, just keep working. Building. Running. Whatever we're called to do.

It's simple and it's powerful.

You may not feel like doing it. You may feel tired, discouraged, and doubtful you're even doing the right thing. Keep building. *Never* stop building. But can I tell you something?

The point at which you're most ready to quit is likely the turning point in your rebuilding effort. There are so many people who quit just as the momentum is beginning to build. Applied force over a period of time starts to create momentum, and once you have momentum, it's hard to stop. And when you reach the halfway point, it may grow harder, but you're almost over the hump. You've never been closer to gathering momentum and breaking through.

How long do you think it took for Nehemiah and the people to rebuild the wall that surrounded the city of Jerusalem?

The answer is fifty-two days, according to Nehemiah 6:15.

Somehow that doesn't seem so long. Yet life is like that. All the obstacles seem epic; we might have expected decades of work. But sometimes, when we look back, we realize we didn't have so far to go. The real obstacle was how we saw it.

Don't give in. Don't give up. Keep on praying and building. You may be fifty-two short, praying, working, persevering days from the breakthrough of your life.

9

One Step at a Time

I try to ask the big questions—the questions others don't dare ask. Such as, Why can't we tickle ourselves?* Why do just your fingers and your toes crinkle up in the bathtub? And male nipples: What's the story there?†

This book got me thinking, What about marathons? Why are they 26.2 miles? I googled it. It turns out that the original Greek guy (the one preachers always refer to) ran about twenty-five miles from Marathon to Athens to announce the defeat of the Persians. His name was Pheidippides, which even Greeks had trouble spelling. When he got to Athens, he said, "Niki!" Which meant, "Victory!" Then he suddenly dropped in his tracks and died.

When the Olympics were revived in 1898, the distance for a marathon was set at about twenty-five miles as a tribute to that guy, though more the finishing part than the keeling

---

* Try it. You know you want to.
† I'm not adding male nipples to things that wrinkle in the bathtub; I'm questioning the purpose of their existence.

over and dying part. But in 1908, the Olympics were in London. The course was Windsor Castle to White City Stadium, which came out to twenty-six miles. But they had to add 385 yards to the end of it so that the racers would run right up to the royal family. Not that the royal family could be bothered to walk a few yards themselves, of course. That wouldn't be royal.

Organizers argued about the length of the run for another decade or so, but to make a long story short, 26.2 stuck. Even if the royal family isn't attending your particular marathon, it's still going to be 26.2 miles.

The greatest runners in the world will tell you it's not a distance you can sprint, even if you lop off those last 385 yards. This is a distance run. The finish line is too far away to see. Instead, you focus on one step at a time.

Your next question, surely, is how many steps does the average runner take when running a marathon?

I'll be honest, my math skills are lacking. That's one of the reasons I became a pastor. People sometimes ask me if there was a moment I knew I was called to ministry. It was definitely when I found out there's no geometry at seminary. It was like I could hear God's voice. That was my burning bush. But let me take a stab at putting the number of steps a person takes when running a marathon into a word problem:

Jimmy decides he wants to run a marathon. A marathon is a 26.2 mile race. There are 63,360 inches in a mile. Each stride Jimmy takes covers 30 inches. How many steps will Jimmy take to run a marathon? Show your work.*

* 63,360 x 26.2 = 1,660,032 inches. 1,660,032 / 30 = if you said 55,334 steps, you were correct!

In short, it's plain that Jimmy will be a tired boy and will wish he'd been in a simpler word problem, maybe with having several apples and giving a couple away.

Today, of course, we use all kinds of apps and devices to track our steps. If you're running for distance and begin to feel a cramp in your right calf, then look at your pedometer and find you've gone 12,237 steps—you're going to be discouraged.

My friend Wesley Korir runs marathons competitively. He's won the Los Angeles Marathon twice and even won the famed Boston Marathon. One afternoon, I met him at the park on a beautiful day to go for a run (if there is such a thing). I asked him what he tells himself when he's exhausted and doesn't want to keep going. He replied there are always some unexpected challenges. It may be a cooler or hotter climate than what he's accustomed to. Three or four miles in, he might be dealing with some unexpected pain in his foot. He may not be keeping the pace he knows he needs to keep. He explained that when he feels discouraged, or when it's a struggle to keep going, he often tells himself two things.

The first thing he tells himself is *One step at a time. Just take the next step.*

Focusing on 55,334 steps when you're tired and hurting would make finishing the race seem impossible. If you just take the next step, and then the next step, and then the next, you'll eventually cross the finish line. The apostle Paul puts it this way: "Let us not become weary in doing good, for at the proper time we will reap a harvest if we do not give up" (Gal. 6:9).

Paul would often use imagery of running a race, but here he uses agricultural language. If we keep sowing, even when we feel weary and worn out, it will be worth it. So, to mix our metaphors, if you take one step at a time and if you do not give up, eventually you'll reap a harvest.*

Keep taking one step at a time, and at the proper time you'll discover a cumulative effect. The word *cumulative* could be defined as a gradual building up. It's not something that happens all at once but something that happens little by little. Eventually the race we run is made up of tens of thousands of individual steps. Each step, in the moment, may seem insignificant, but the cumulative effect of all the steps ultimately determines what race we ran.

The real reason many of us give up on running the race is we underestimate the importance of one step at a time. Focusing on intentionally taking the next step and then the next step and then the next step is the secret to not giving up. Just take the next step.

Let's apply the power of intentionally taking the next step to an area where many people give up: finances. Let's imagine that you turn forty years old and suddenly realize you haven't really saved any money for retirement. You would love to retire by age seventy, but you do the math and realize you're going to need at least a quarter of a million dollars to retire. That number seems impossible. What's the point of even trying?

You reluctantly meet with a financial advisor, even though it feels like the only way to get from where you are to where you need to be is by winning the lottery or perhaps robbing a bank.

---

* Just imagine an Olympic marathon runner scattering seeds right and left as he runs. Soon the track will be surrounded by tall cornstalks, and you won't be able to see who wins.

The financial advisor instead shows you the power of compound interest and challenges you to start investing today. She points out that saving the five bucks a day you spend on coffee will add up. If you invest that sum and average a 5 percent rate of return, in thirty years you will have saved $125,000. If you could manage to save ten bucks a day, you would have over a quarter of a million dollars.

Saving ten bucks today may not seem like you've done much, but that's the power of the cumulative effect.

When we're up against what feels like a big challenge, there's a tendency to think we need a big solution. We're looking for one big decision that can help get us out of a big dilemma. In reality, the key to persevering is to focus on one step at a time.

The First Step

There's an old saying: "The first step is the hardest." I don't know who said that, but it was probably someone who knew how many steps made a marathon.

Often we're ready to give up because we're thinking of how far the journey will be. We end up quitting before we even take the first step. In our modern society, not only is it easy to get married but it's even easier to get divorced. Just as quickly as couples can jump into marriage without helpful guidance, married couples can separate with the same level of guidance—none.

I'm curious to know how many people go ahead and get a divorce without praying seriously, reading a book on marriage, talking to friends or family about the decision, or meeting with a counselor or marriage therapist. Sadly, I'd guess most people fail to mount a serious, thoughtful effort. Maybe they see the size of the task and it seems too huge. Maybe they take counsel of their emotions rather than clear, logical thinking.

One of the reasons we don't end up taking the first step until it feels too late is because we have had good intentions of taking that first step for a long time. Ask anyone whose weight has spiraled out of control, and they'll tell you they didn't mean for it to happen. Countless times they've told themselves they were going to make changes. Week after week they promised themselves they were going to get on top of it. They had good intentions, but now it feels too late.

Good intentions have a way of making us feel like we've done something when we haven't really done anything. We pat ourselves on the back for having good intentions, but we've never actually taken a first step.

I read an article a few months ago that talked about the growing popularity of people wearing workout clothes but not actually working out. There's a category of clothing called "athleisure" that has exploded into a hundred-billion-dollar industry. You probably noticed that the word *athleisure* is a combination of *athletic* and *leisure*. You may have also noticed it only contains a part of the word *athletic* while including all of the word *leisure*. That's not a coincidence.

There are millions of people wearing yoga pants who aren't in fact doing yoga. One of the reasons athleisure clothing has become so popular is that, by wearing it, we feel better about ourselves. We may not actually get around to working out, but the fact that we have good intentions and are ready to work out makes us feel like we've worked out—when all we've really done is get dressed.

Don't convince yourself that your good intentions are the first step. You can have good intentions and never move an inch forward.

You can have good intentions of making things right with a friend or family member whom you've hurt, but until you actually have a conversation, you haven't done anything. You can have good intentions of losing weight, but your good intentions won't cancel out the cheese fries you had for lunch.

You can have good intentions of reconnecting with God, but until you're willing to disconnect from Netflix and social media from time to time, your good intentions won't matter. You can have good intentions of affirming your love to your wife on your anniversary, but those intentions won't cause her to overlook the fact that you forgot to get her anything.

There's actually a psychological term for this phenomenon. It's called the "intention-action gap." The idea is that most of us live our lives in the gap between intention and action. Lingering in the procrastination zone is a way of giving up without actually saying it.

I recently read an example of how our actions don't necessarily align with our intentions. Netflix used to ask its users what we wanted to watch in the future. Based on each user's response, Netflix would create a list of possible future programs. Maybe new documentaries were all over our list, so Netflix would create a list of documentaries we might be interested in.

But at some point, Netflix realized asking people what they intended to watch was not a good indicator of what people would actually watch. Intention: a documentary on science. Action: early '90s Adam Sandler movie. Netflix actually announced that its users had watched half a billion

Sandler movies.[1] And no, *Napoleon Dynamite* doesn't count as a documentary on Emperor Napoleon of France.

We have one set of ideas about how our life is going to go, another set of actions about where it does go. It's not a matter of dishonesty; these are real intentions. We imagine ourselves living the kind of life we believe should be lived. But life is so daily—it's built on momentary decisions, day after day, action after action. Maybe later I'll watch that documentary on good digestion my cousin raves about. Right now, I think I'll watch that episode of *The Office*.*

From Good Intentions to Intentional

Running the race requires staunch discipline. At any moment, the easy move is to stop and catch your breath. But you know that if you keep making the easy moves, you'll never win the race. Moment by moment, we need to align actions with intentions.

When Jesus called his disciples to follow him, each one faced a moment of decision. In Luke 9:23, Jesus issued an invitation for all who might follow him. Would-be followers needed to pick up a cross every day and keep walking. The hardest part of that is the *every day*. It doesn't happen by accident.

The disciples had to walk away with Jesus, then and there. And everything about life as they knew it had to change. Fishing nets, a tax collector's booth, family and friends—these were the things they knew. They had to give themselves completely to a whole new world that Jesus set out for them.

* The one where Michael burns his foot while using his George Foreman grill to cook bacon in bed. Classic.

After Jesus issues his invitation, a man comes to him and expresses a desire to follow him. He says to Jesus, "I will follow you wherever you go" (v. 57). He has every intention of doing that. Whatever the course, he'll run it. Jesus replies that even the animals—foxes and birds—have homes, but he, Jesus, makes his home in the will of God. That's a life lived completely outside the comfort zone. The man has good intentions, but he's just not ready to give up his safety net.

In high school, our basketball coach hated cutting players. Instead, he got players to cut themselves. He'd set a trash can in each of the four corners of the gym, then run us until people started puking.* He knew that by the time the first official practice came, the group would have been winnowed down from a mob to just a few dedicated athletes.

Most of us don't need to be cut from God's team—we give up all on our own.

And remember, *race* and *agony* are synonyms. "Run the agony set out for you." What is your agony? What good intentions have you struggled to make good on—and could it be that the reason for falling short was your comfort zone, your lack of willingness to be disciplined?

It could be little things, like reading to the kids at night after you had a really hard day of work. Maybe it's saying you're sorry after an argument, when an apology would mend things and a delay would make them worse.

Maybe it's admitting you wronged someone when they don't necessarily know you did. Maybe it's reaching out to that coworker who needs encouragement, although your boss has been equally hard on you.

* Millennials: this was back in the day when the principal would spank you. Not metaphorically or verbally, but physically take a paddle and spank you.

When you look at the race you're running, what is it that keeps you from moving from good intentions to action?

Accidental to Intentional

Sometimes accidents get in the way of good intentions.

Recently I was traveling in Haiti. I needed to get from the Port-au-Prince airport to a town called Jacmel. The drive goes through the mountains on what could loosely be described as "roads." But an American pilot who lives there said he could fly me in his four-seater plane and get me to Jacmel in fifteen minutes. The pilot was named Roger, which I loved because I got to sit in the cockpit and say, "Roger, Roger" whenever he asked me a question. I'm sure he enjoyed this dynamic as much as I did, even if he didn't let on.

The plane was around forty years old, and a number of the gauges didn't seem to be working. The flight over the mountains was pretty rough, and there were times when the mountains were higher than we were, which feels a little—what's the word? *Disconcerting*.

In the middle of the flight, Roger started telling me about the time he made a crash landing. I gathered it was successful. He pointed out to me where the plane went down; he said there was a complete engine failure. I asked what happened to the plane, and that's when Roger said, "We're flying in it right now."

Among the conversations that you don't want to have with your pilot while you're midair is the story about him crash-landing the plane that you're currently flying in. I wasn't sure how to respond.

I finally asked, "Well, did you get it fixed?"

"Yeah, I did all the work myself."

I felt a little better. Then he added, "You know, you can't get all the tools you need in Haiti; you just make do."

Again I was at a loss, and again I asked a question that only seemed to make things worse. "Did you ever figure out what went wrong?"

And Roger said, "You know, I'm not really sure. Sometimes accidents happen."

"Accidents happen" is not the phrase you want your pilot to use when explaining what caused the crash landing of the plane you're in. We're not talking about bad intentions—nobody did it on purpose. "Accidents happen" is what we say when something went wrong but we don't want to feel bad about it. We had good intentions, but accidents happen. Appropriate times to say accidents happen:

- When you knock over a lamp.
- When you've left a door unlocked.
- When you break a dish in the kitchen.
- When you scratch a bumper on a speed bump.

Inappropriate times to say accidents happen:

- When you've had an affair.
- When you've been an absent father.
- When you get to the end of your life and try to explain some of your existence.
- When you crash-land your plane.

In Galatians 6:9, Paul says we shouldn't grow weary, because there's a harvest to reap if we don't give up. Leading up to that verse, he mentions the law of sowing and reaping. We reap what we sow regardless of intent. The seeds can be knocked out of your hand accidentally, but they grow where they fall just the same. "God cannot be mocked," Paul writes. "A man reaps what he sows" (v. 7).

In other words, it's a little like the law of gravity. You might say, "I didn't vote for that law. I'm staunchly antigravity. Repeal gravity! Down with gravity!"*

Doesn't matter; it's the law. I was very much antigravity when I heard about the plane crash, but there was nothing I could do about it. In the same way, we reap what we sow, accident or not.

Is there such a thing as a seed store? Let's picture it as a candy store, just with seeds. Though I'm guessing the farmer uses Amazon like everybody else these days. Anyway, the farmer walks down the aisle of the seed store and fills his shopping bag from the various bins randomly. When the harvest comes, he's going to find out what seeds he selected. The point is, select carefully. Plant intentionally.

Accidental lives seem fun and spontaneous to some—just throw the dice every day and see what you land on. But when the harvest comes due, you'll likely wish you'd put time and thought into your future.

Hard Habit to Break

Another problem with intentionality is the deep ruts we create when we run the same old path over and over; grooves form below our feet. Repeated actions create an orderly

---

* See what I did there?

pattern over time. Then we get stuck in them. When we finally make an attempt to get out, it's too difficult and we give up.

This phenomenon is known as *automaticity*. What this means is that we can easily move into muscle memory routines that don't require much thought—such as driving a car, walking, or breathing—without really thinking about it. This is because at one time, one way or another, we created these habits. Since these habits don't require much focused thought, say, like an algebra problem, they can be done subconsciously, without even thinking about it—such as when you turn right instead of left out of your cul-de-sac without even thinking, because that's how you drive to work. Our habits are hard to break.

God never chooses a used groove in your life. He marks out a whole new course. We have to be intentional about keeping his plan in the forefront of our thinking, so spiritual "muscle memory" never eases us off course. It's so easy to fall into old patterns and mistake their comfort for what we should be doing.

Maybe you grew up with a mother who was very reactive. She would deal with stress and conflict by yelling and becoming physical. You swore to yourself you would never be like that. You despised the path she was on, yet without even meaning to, you have found yourself reacting the same way. You recognize a situation, perhaps even subconsciously, and respond with what feels appropriate. Even if you always hated it, it's what you know, and the mind seeks a familiar pattern.

Maybe you grew up with a father who was passive. When things were difficult at home, your dad just checked out emotionally. He worked long hours and seemed to disappear for days at a time. Or maybe he was there, but he wasn't really there. He would kick back in the recliner, watch TV, and no one was supposed to bother him.

When you got married and started a family, you swore you were going to do things differently. You were going to engage and connect. And every once in a while, when you're driving home late from work, you remember that commitment and tell yourself, *It's just a busy season right now. I'll start being more intentional with my kids when they get a little older.*

But how long have you been saying that? You are stuck in the gap between intention and action.

If you've ever been extremely out of shape, then decided to get in shape, you know how hard it is to break past patterns. You try to change your diet, but your body is addicted to sugar. You try to start exercising, but your body begs to differ; it really enjoys a lack of exercise.

After you watch what you eat and work out for three or four days, past patterns try to take back lost ground. However, if you can stick with it for just a few weeks, what felt so unnatural starts to feel more natural. You just have to win that transition period between the old patterns and the new.

I have a friend who is a personal trainer. As a rule, I try not to have friends who are personal trainers, but he was my friend first. I was talking to him about how he helps people who are struggling to break old habits. I asked, "What do you say to your clients when they're struggling to keep their commitment? What do you say when they feel like giving up?"

He said, "I simply tell them, 'Just show up.' Those three words disrupt old patterns."

He went on to give me some examples. "When they call and say, 'I'm really tired today' or 'I don't think I can do it today,' my answer to them is always the same: 'Just show up.'"

In fact, hanging on the wall of his gym is a sign with big, bold letters that reads: JUST SHOW UP.

Just showing up makes a statement to the body. It says, *I'm here. I'm not doing things the way I have always done them. I'm not giving up!*

What Showing Up Looks Like

A number of months ago, I got an email from a man in our community who is not a member of our church. He actually doesn't attend any church. But he was dying, and he didn't have much time left.

At one point in his life, while lying in bed, he'd turned on the TV and watched one of our services, which prompted him to reach out and ask if I'd come visit him. So I went to his house for a visit. It was clear to me immediately that he was running his final lap in this life. He wasn't in a mood to waste time. He explained that when he was a child, he'd become a Christian—but for the last number of decades, he'd run away from God. Now he realized he needed to get things right. Was that possible? He looked up at me with a question mark in his eyes.

"Do you have a Bible?" I asked.

I don't tend to bring a Bible on calls like these; I like to see theirs. There's something about seeing someone's Bible that tells me who I'm talking to. A snapshot of the race they've run is right in front of me.

The man started to say that no, he didn't. Then he broke off, pointed across the room at a coffee table, and said, "Look there."

There I found a huge Bible, one of those gigantic, pulpit-sized King James Bibles from back in the day. I wasn't even sure I could pick it up without hurting myself. I was careful to lift with my legs. But I opened the book, and dust filled the air around me. I ignored that, turned to a few Gospel passages about Jesus, then flipped to Romans and read the verses about sin and salvation.

I asked him if he needed to get right with God before he died.

When you know you're coming to the end, the gap between intention and action tends to close rapidly. Anything important—now is the time. The man began to express this very idea as he spoke of his life. He'd finally had certain conversations, apologizing to his daughter and offering forgiveness to his ex. He'd finally written some letters of gratitude, finally gotten relationships in order. All his financial issues were handled. This man was getting his house in order. Yet still, in the back of his mind, there was a glaring intention that had been there for years: *At some point, I must get right with God.*

Those intentions may have been as old as I was at that point. They may have followed him through every transition of life, through relationships, through the lifespan of hopes and dreams and fears. They never went away, those intentions. They never gave up, since God never gives up. This man never quite did either.

The course God has laid out is always right in front of us. It begins that very moment. When the man understood that it wasn't too late, that Jesus had made all things right, he wept. All he needed to do was say yes and mean it. He did. He confessed his sins. He repented with a sincerity that couldn't have been mistaken. And I saw him walk, like a joyful child, into the kingdom, a new life beginning from a dying one.

When I got back to the office, I mailed him a Bible in an easier translation—a Bible he could pick up with his weakening arms, one he could read and grasp. In his final days, it was always by his side.

He'd put it off forever. He'd made wrong choices. But eventually he decided to show up, and that's all that was required of him. He showed up by sending me one simple email, and it changed his eternity.

...

The second thing Wesley, my marathon-running friend, tells himself is *The finish line is closer than you think.* One step at a time, and the finish line is closer than you think. If you are tired and worn out, would you tell yourself those two things?

10

Keep Your Confidence

How would you like an opportunity to train with one of the most elite fighting forces in the modern world?

I was invited by text to do just that. My friend, who has some connections at a military base nearby, was reaching out to me. I can't tell you where, what elite force, or what the mission was—top secret, you understand. Highly classified. As a matter of fact, I've probably already said too much. This info doesn't leave this book. Is that understood?

About a half-dozen of my buddies were going to be a part of this exercise. We were civilians, but in our minds we formed an elite, specially chosen unit coming together to help our special forces train for, you know, world-saving stuff. I figured my part in the training exercise wouldn't be too physically demanding. I'd stand on the sidelines, like at a football game, and make some kind of brilliant observation for the good of national security.

As the time grew closer, I began hearing stories that indicated the experience might be a little more hands-on than

I thought. We'd be playing the part of enemy combatants. When the special forces team attacked, my group would fight back and drive them out. Wow! The six of us on our team began to text back and forth, talking a little trash, boasting about our personal exploits of valor and courage.

At some point, I noticed that we were using a lot of emojis in this text stream, which is a little disconcerting. As a general rule, if your emoji game is on point, you're less likely to have the machismo for special forces combat. I'll admit, that got me thinking. Then, when we arrived at the military base, we signed waiver after waiver—which, all by itself, pointed toward death or dismemberment. It was at this point that things became more real, and my courage sprang a small leak.

None of us spoke it aloud, but all of us had the look that said, *What have I gotten myself into?*

We geared up, meaning we'd be facing arguably the most elite group of warriors in the modern world, wearing skateboard pads and armed with paintball guns. My courage sprang a second, more insistent leak.

We rode in the back of a pickup truck to what looked like a third-world village after heavy conflict. As we got out of the truck, one of the guys I was with said, "I really think we can win this thing, guys." But his voice cracked up into Mickey Mouse range as he said it. The message I got from it was actually, *We're in big trouble. Let's keep our eyes peeled for a good place to hide.*

We were then separated and put into different houses, where we were instructed to wait for the special forces team to show up so we could engage them.

As I stared through a broken window into the darkness of night, I lost a little more courage. Suddenly, out of nowhere, a half-dozen Chinook and Blackhawk helicopters flew in with no lights. Dozens of soldiers wearing night vision goggles rappelled out of the helicopters. Several cars in the street exploded as if hit with rocket launchers.

I later learned that the whole village had been rigged with pyrotechnics. There were explosions taking place all around us, including the top of the house I was in. The air was filled with gunfire. I knew they were firing sim rounds, but it didn't sound too "sim."

Then came the flashbangs. A nine-banger was thrown into the abandoned house I was in, and it was at this point that instinct took over. Without making any conscious decision to do so, I found myself running away and looking for something to dive under.

I've often wondered over the years if I was a fight guy or a flight guy. Now I know.

Here's what that experience taught me. My courage is only as real as my confidence. When my confidence is exposed, my courage evaporates. I had no confidence, because I had no training, no conditioning, no expertise, no high-tech equipment. I didn't arrive by Chinook; I arrived by Chevy.

When my courage was tested, my confidence was measured and found wanting. Strength and courage are directly related to whether your confidence is legit.

Take Courage

The message of this book has been pretty simple: don't give up; take courage.

That same challenge echoes through page after page of the Bible. People in every kind of situation are told to take courage and resist fear. But how? Where is courage found? If you think about the situations in your own life, you'll see that it's always rooted in something real—never in emotion or hopes or any kind of smoke and mirrors.

Have you ever been told to "be brave" or to "take courage" without being given a reason? A child is scared of the darkness. His dad impatiently says, "Be a big boy—be brave!" That doesn't really help much for most kids. But it might help if Dad comes into the bedroom, sits down, and offers a dose of reasoning before showing there's no monster in the closet. It helps when Dad says, "I'll be right nearby, just in the next room, and I will always be there for you."

We need a sturdy source of confidence. Like everything else, courage is a construct built on some kind of foundation. Give someone all the money from a Monopoly game and send them shopping. The whole thing falls apart at the first cash register, because nothing is behind that money.

I talk to people who began coming to church in their forties. What they often tell me is that they felt confident about life until they went through their first real test—a lost job, a very sick child. Turned out their confidence had no foundation. It burst like a pretty bubble. That's when they realized they needed something deeper, something that penetrated to the soul, and they sought it in God.

The writer of Hebrews doesn't suggest any sketchy courage or confidence. The whole book is based on the supremacy of Christ—how, in comparison after comparison, he is better than anything people have clutched or depended upon. He is a solid foundation.

We don't give up because, no matter what we're facing, Jesus is better. No matter how deep the hole, Jesus is deeper.

No matter how dark the prognosis, Jesus brings light that chases the darkness away. We "[fix] our eyes on Jesus," as Hebrews 12:2 puts it. When you're facing a frightening situation, you fix your eyes on your source of strength. Children look to their parents. Players look to their coaches. Citizens turn to their leaders in times of crisis.

Looking inside ourselves won't get it done. We remember Stuart Smalley, the *Saturday Night Live* character who peered into a mirror and told himself, "I'm good enough, I'm smart enough, and doggone it, people like me." We wish we could tell him it was going to work. Courage must be based on something powerful, something outside ourselves.

So when I say "Take courage," I don't mean the superficial, emotional imitation. I don't mean staring at yourself in a mirror and getting psyched by telling yourself things that aren't true. I don't mean listening to a workout playlist and getting hyped up. It must be based in a confidence that is well-constructed.

That word, *confidence*, appears a number of times in Hebrews 10–13. The message is that it's found in Christ. The original audience for this letter went into battle confident and self-assured, but things got a little scary. Life threw some flashbang grenades, and they began running the race—in the opposite direction.

Hebrews 10:32–34 tells us they'd started the race with courage and determination. "Remember those earlier days," the writer says. They'd gone through plenty of abuse. They'd suffered. Some of them had been thrown in prison; others had seen their property confiscated. But they'd held out because they had "better and lasting possessions."

In other words, "You can haul away our widescreen TVs and expensive golf clubs. What you can't take from us are our riches in Christ. You can beat us, even kill us, but you can't take away our eternal life. Christ is superior."

That was in the early days, when their faith was new and they were bold and resilient. Now they were growing tired. The battle was wearing them down. And the writer urges them, "Do not throw away your confidence; it will be richly rewarded" (v. 35).

He's asking, What has really changed? Is Christ less sufficient now? Have his blessings faded in some way? He is still there for you. Eternal life is still eternal. You may walk away from your faith, but it will never walk away from you.

Courage falters when we shift from Jesus to something or someone else. We start to wonder if Jesus really is better. Maybe you went away to college and you thought, *I don't know if Jesus is better. I've been told he's better my entire life, but now I'm out on my own. I'm seeing some things that look pretty good.* And you walked away from the confidence you had in Jesus and began to put it in other things. It seemed to work just fine—until life threw a flashbang in your house.

Don't throw away your confidence. It's your confidence in Christ that will give you the courage to endure and not give up. So grab hold of that with both hands and don't let go.

Let's identitfy a few of the ways we throw away our confidence and become discouraged and lose heart.

Considering Circumstances Rather Than Christ

The writer urges us, "Consider him who endured such opposition from sinners, so that you will not grow weary and lose heart" (Heb. 12:3).

That phrase *lose heart* is also translated as "discouraged" or, even more literally, "so that you will not lose courage." These Christians were losing courage because life had not turned out the way they had hoped.

When you put your confidence in your circumstances and your circumstances don't go as planned, your confidence is shaken. You thought your health would be better, your marriage would be better, your job would be better, your children would be better, your finances would be better.

Lewis Smedes writes about Tammy Kramer, who was chief of the outpatient AIDS clinic at Los Angeles County Hospital. She was watching a young man who had come in one morning for his regular dose of medicine. He sat in tired silence on a high stool while a new doctor at the clinic poked a needle into his side. Without looking up at his face, the doctor asked, "You are aware, aren't you, that you are not long for this world—a year at most?"

The patient stopped at Tammy's desk on his way out, face distorted in pain, and hissed, "That SOB did away with my hope."

Tammy responded, "I guess he did. Maybe it's time to find another one."[1]

But is there another hope? When you discover that what you've put your hope and confidence in has disappointed you, remember that Jesus is better.

Hebrews says that when your confidence is shaken and your courage is slipping, consider Jesus. What does it mean to consider? It means what you would assume it means: to contemplate. To think about.

Spend some time thinking about what Jesus did for you on the cross; how he endured suffering for you. Instead of "considering Jesus," we have a tendency to "consider our circumstances." We think about and contemplate what we are going through. We give our thoughts to challenges and difficulties. We focus on what isn't fair. We fixate on our frustration. We obsess over our obstacles.

When we bypass all that and intentionally consider what Jesus endured on the cross, it gives us confidence that we too can endure.

The word *consider* also means to compare. Throughout the book of Hebrews, Jesus is compared to different people and different things to make the point that he is always better. Intentionally comparing Jesus can restore your confidence and hope.

Compare Jesus to your addiction, to your debt, to your illness, to your boss, to your past failures, to your future fears. Then consider, "Is Jesus better?"

Another way to compare is to look at what you're going through in comparison to what *he* went through for you. When you're discouraged and losing heart, consider what Jesus did. Visualize the whole process, from his agony in the garden, knowing he would have to be crucified for you, to his trial, his abuse, his long walk up the hill with a wooden cross on his shoulders, and finally those hours of pain he suffered on your behalf. Put yourself in the story. Realize he did it *for you*.

I read about a guy named Joe Lee, who ran a 150-mile ultramarathon through the Sahara Desert. It makes me thirsty just writing that. His wife, Allison, had died of cancer about a year and a half earlier, and his run was raising money for the American Cancer Society.

After the first day of brutal conditions, a number of runners had already been airlifted out. He reached the eighty-mile mark and, because of the heat, the soles of his shoes blew out, which I didn't even know was possible. So he had very little protection as he was running through the Sahara. His feet became very blistered, and every step was excruciatingly painful.

When he finished the race four days later, he was asked how he was able to endure through such pain and exhaustion.

He said, "I thought about Allison a lot. This is nothing compared to what she went through."[2]

Consider. Compare. Perspective tends to put the mind right where it should be. When you're tired and ready to give up, think about Jesus and say to yourself, *This is nothing compared to what he went through.*

And keep running your race.

Confusing Confidence

Another way we throw away our confidence is by confusing our confidence in ourselves with confidence in Christ. I don't think we even realize how often we do this.

This confusion is especially prevalent in the Western world, where we're discipled in the school of self-confidence. We're taught to believe in ourselves, and that we can be anything we want to be. We're given courage to go out into the world because of this confidence. We're told, "Believe it and achieve it. The sky's the limit for your potential!"

That psyches us up; it makes us rush into the world like conquerors, and it's great. Until it isn't, which comes pretty soon. What's it really based on? Eventually, self-confidence gets exposed. We are forced to acknowledge that we don't have what it takes. Something happens, and we can't get around the fact that we *can't* achieve it just by believing it. The sky's *not* the limit for our potential.

Your potential is about like most other people's, actually. Somebody told you you're "one in a million," and that's true. But so is that guy over here. And that girl over there. And all of the other ones out of that million. Everybody in a million is one in a million, right? So what really, truly sets us apart?

I was recently reading about a dating website that revealed how thousands of its users had answered one particular question on their compatibility survey. The users of the dating website were asked, "Are you a genius?"

According to the results, close to 50 percent of a certain gender said yes to that question. About half of the men on the dating website confirmed their genius status. Now, statistically speaking, about one in one thousand would actually be geniuses. So that means five out of ten men think they're one in a thousand. How do you make sense of this statistical anomaly? My guess is that the majority of those men have a confidence in themselves that has never been tested.

If your confidence is in yourself, eventually that confidence will be tested and found wanting. Some of you know exactly what I'm talking about, because you once got by on self-confidence just fine. That worked great for you, until the day of the big confidence test.

It worked great until you got the diagnosis from the doctor. It worked great until your wife said it was over. It worked great until you walked into a room of family and friends gathered for your intervention. It worked great until you discovered his secret text messages. It worked great until you heard the word *autistic*. It worked great until you found yourself filing for unemployment. It worked great until kids started bullying you online because of your beliefs, or your coworkers started to ostracize you because your commitment felt like an indictment on their compromise.

At some point in this race, if your confidence is in yourself, you will be exposed.

Think about this for a second. What would you say destroys people's confidence the most? If you just had to pick one thing, what would you say?

Maybe it would help to put some context around the question. What would you say destroys a professional athlete's confidence? Do a little research on this and you'll find a repeated theme: *failure*.

When you fail, it's hard to get that out of your mind the next time you try. If you didn't succeed the last time, it's that much harder to find the courage to do it the next time. Spiritually this is true as well. If our confidence is in ourselves, we may start the race strong, but after a few falls on the track, our failures start to take their toll.

Hebrews repeatedly makes the case that our courage doesn't come from a confidence in ourselves or our words. Our confidence is not in what we've done but what has been done on our account. Hebrews 10:19 says that we have confidence to enter the "Most Holy Place" (as in the ancient temple) by a new way—the blood of Jesus. Whereas there was a curtain that marked the boundary in the temple, and no one but the high priest could cross it, the body of Jesus, broken for us, gives us entry. We can go in boldly to be washed by the high priest, Jesus himself. We can have the "full assurance that faith brings" (v. 22).

For the early readers, those words meant a lot. The idea of entering the holiest part of the temple was mind-boggling.

And with Jesus as high priest, Jesus there to cleanse us, Jesus to give us new strength—how could we fear? How could we not have confidence? He made a way for us.

Take Heart

I love the command from Scripture to "take heart." It's for those who are losing heart.

On the surface, these words don't seem very helpful. They're nice to say, perhaps to stitch onto a pillow and take to the nursing home. But telling someone who is losing heart to "take heart" is like telling someone who is hungry not to be hungry. It's like telling that frightened child to be brave.

But when the Bible tells us to take heart, it's not a call to have confidence in ourselves but to have confidence in God, based not on some contrived self-confidence but on confidence in who God is.

Hebrews 11 mentions a character from the Old Testament who learned to take heart. His name is Gideon, and we read about him in Judges 6. In Judges, Israel is constantly under the thumb of some other nation. In this case, it's the Midianites. They've driven many Israelites to hide in hills and caves. The people cry out to God, as they do in each of the episodes in Judges—and God sends a "judge," a deliverer.

The angel comes to Gideon to tell him he'll be that judge this time. Gideon, like everyone else, is laying low. He's threshing wheat in a winepress. "The LORD is with you, mighty warrior," the angel says (Judges 6:12).

Think about this. Gideon is hiding out, but God sees him as a mighty warrior. Gideon immediately tells the angel all the reasons he's not up to the task. Just like Moses told God.

Just like you and I do. He has no courage because he has no confidence—he's the weakest of a weak family, he points out. Here am I, send somebody else.

Maybe you'd expect God to say, "Listen, Gideon, I believe in you. Dig down deep! Find the right stuff inside yourself. You can do it!" There is no montage of Gideon going into fight training while the up-tempo soundtrack plays. No psych-up. The coach doesn't come in for a halftime pep talk. None of that. God just says five little words: "I will be with you" (v. 16).

Gideon takes with him three hundred men and some very poor excuses for weaponry, and he destroys a vast Midianite army. Sometimes people teach the story as being about Gideon's military cleverness, but it's not—it's about the power of God, and Gideon finding his confidence in that rather than himself.

As a matter of fact, any excess confidence in himself or his abilities would have ruined the whole thing. We have to be delivered from all that and learn to have courage based on confidence in God. "The Lord is my helper; I will not be afraid" (Heb. 13:6).

I have a problem with this at certain, predictable times: Saturday night, after preaching that evening's service, and before the Sunday morning service. Sometimes (too many times) it doesn't go as well as I'd hoped on Saturday night, and then I have to face preaching that same sermon again the next morning. I usually pray my way through it, and the Holy Spirit gives me the strength I need. But on occasion, a few times a year, I am crippled by feelings of inadequacy. I get up on Sunday morning with feelings of dread, frightened, my confidence shot. Ready to run away and find a place to hide.

Why? Because Saturday night exposed me. I leaned on my expertise and found out how foolish it is to do that. Every now and then, God needs to strip away the illusions and show us where the power is coming from—and where we can't afford to rely upon it to come from.

When that moment comes, I gently wake my wife and tell her it's one of those mornings. I'm not up to this. I don't want to do this.

Some spouses would say, "Oh, honey, just get your mind off it. You'll be fine. Go back to sleep." She doesn't do that, nor does she say, "Honey, you're the best! Believe in yourself. You're brilliant and dynamic and sexy."

She doesn't say anything directly to me, as a matter of fact. She speaks to God.

My wife takes my hands in hers and begins to pray God's truth over me. Her words remind me to lift up my eyes to where my help comes from. She reminds me my faith is built on nothing less than Jesus and his righteousness. Not me. She helps me seize God's charge to Joshua, to be strong and courageous, because I go in the name of the Lord. Not my name. I matter only as much as the glove that contains the hand. The life and power and vitality come from the hand of God. A glove is just a glove is just a glove, and I'm just a glove.

There is something incredibly freeing about being a glove.

Jesus is better than my preparation, he is better than my observations, he is better than my delivery, and he is better than the approval of my audience. He is also better than anyone's disapproval.

He's better for you too. Better than anything you can buy, anything you can add to your portfolio. He's better than any website or relationship, any new fad or approach. He's better than anything. He is better than being ruled by worry over your problems, better than serving another hour of slavery to the impulses and temptations that bring you down.

He's better than accepting a marriage that isn't what God designed it to be, a job that isn't glorifying him in the way you know it could, or a family that isn't thriving in the power of his special presence and blessing.

He is better than your past, better than your present, and better than the most wonderful future you can imagine.

Spend some time looking for occasions in the Bible when we're told, in so many words, to take heart. A favorite of mine is John 16, where Jesus prepares his disciples for the approaching hour of his departure. He knows their limitations. He knows there's nothing at all these puzzled, often stumbling individuals could do to change the world—or even the neighborhood—if left to their own devices. Not to mention the troubles, the hardship, the intense persecution they'll face. The odds against them, humanly speaking, will be about thirty zillion to one.

Jesus isn't worried about any of that. Calmest one in the room. He looks at the sea of anxious faces and says, "I have told you these things, so that in me you may have peace. In this world you will have trouble. But take heart! I have overcome the world" (John 16:33).

Let that sink in. Jesus is better than the world.

I know all about the world and what it throws at you. You have worries, doubts, lapses of confidence. I know you wake up sometimes consumed by sheer fright, paralyzed.

But instead of telling Jesus about your worries, talk back to those worries for a change. Interrupt them. Be downright rude to your worries and tell them about Jesus. Tell them he's better—better than they are, better than the world itself. Worries never last, but Jesus is forever.

Jesus is better. Put your confidence in him. Take heart. Don't give up.

EPILOGUE

Can't Stop. Won't Stop.

I want to make a statement that may seem a little, well—morbid.

At least it's not the kind of thing we often say out loud. I even googled this sentence because I wondered if anyone had ever said it before. I didn't get many hits. While it may not be said out loud, I'm sure I'm not the only one who has ever thought it. Here it is:

Christians die better than anyone.

Admittedly, I haven't done the research to back up this statement, although I think there is plenty of historical data to make a compelling case. I am saying it based on anecdotal evidence, but it would be hard to convince me otherwise.

I remember the first funeral I ever attended. It's the only funeral I remember attending in elementary school. The son of some family friends—let's call him Daniel—was with one of his buddies whom I'll call Shane. There was a tragic accident, and both boys were hit and killed by a train.

The two boys were best friends, so the families agreed to have a double funeral. Daniel's friends and family would sit on one side of the sanctuary, and Shane's friends and family would sit on the other. I sat with my parents toward the back, on Daniel's side.

I remember how I couldn't understand the difference in how the two sides were responding. On Daniel's side, there were certainly tears and grieving. But on Shane's side, the family at times was weeping and wailing loudly. They couldn't find any comfort. Later, I asked my dad why there was such a difference.

My dad explained, "Son, that's the difference Jesus makes. Daniel's family knows that Daniel is in heaven."

I've found this to be true. A few years ago, I walked into a house to say goodbye to my friend Frank. It was a Sunday night, and he was expected to pass within the hour. He was in his own home, where a hospital bed had been set up in the family room. Seven or eight family members were gathered around his bed.

As I approached, I couldn't even see Frank. When I squeezed in between a few of his adult children to see him, I noticed everyone was crying. Everyone but Frank. In fact, he had a rather childlike grin on his face. His son told me he wasn't able to talk, and that the medicine had affected his cognitive abilities. I asked the son, "Do you mind if I pray with him?"

I was given permission, so I knelt beside the bed, took his hand, and began to pray.

In the course of the prayer, he squeezed my hand at certain times. I felt he was understanding me. Afterward, when I looked up, the same childlike smile was on his face. I said, "Frank, why are you smiling?"

"He's not able to process what we're saying," his son explained. But Frank pointed over to a coffee table in the middle of the room. I looked in the direction he was pointing. I didn't see anything that stood out. His son sounded a little more annoyed. "He doesn't understand any of this," he said.

I walked over to the coffee table to find three or four books and a half dozen magazines. But I recognized a book that was peeking out from underneath a few magazines. It was a book I had given to Frank several months earlier, when his health began rapidly declining: *Heaven* by Joni Eareckson Tada. I grabbed it and walked back over to Frank.

"Frank, is this why you're smiling?" I asked, offering him the book. His smile widened, and he put his finger on the word *heaven* there on the cover.

I gently tucked the book between his arm and his body and noticed that everyone had begun to cry again, quietly. Except for Frank. He still had a beautiful smile.

Then, just recently, I went to visit Matt Cappotelli, another man on his way out of this world. He's younger than me. He won a tough man competition on MTV a number of years ago and was a professional wrestler before becoming a personal trainer. My friend the personal trainer I sometimes write about, that's Matt. He was in better physical condition than anyone I knew when he was diagnosed with a malignant brain tumor. He wasted away and eventually had a hard time even forming words to speak.

I stopped by his house and told him I knew it was hard for him to talk, but if he wanted to, I'd be glad to tell him about what heaven would be like. He nodded his head yes. I began to describe what the Bible tells us about heaven: that it will be a place of incredible beauty, perfect rest, delicious food, meaningful tasks, and loving relationships.

At some point, he closed his eyes and rested his head against the back of the chair. His whole body seemed to relax as he listened. As I spoke, I watched tears stream down his cheeks. They were not tears of sadness or fear. I knew exactly what those tears represented: *relief*.

The Finish Line

In the Bible, Paul explains that our present suffering can't be compared to what we will experience in heaven. In 1 Corinthians 2:9, he tells us that no eye has seen, no ear has heard, and no mind has conceived all that God has prepared for those who love him.

Paul had a lot of time to think about the next life. He endured terrible suffering; he was separated from his friends and the work he loved. And he knew that eventually he faced execution by sword. Through all this, his faith gave him the confidence to believe and the courage to keep going until his final breath.

The book of 2 Timothy is the last letter Paul would write before he died. He sits in a cold, bare prison cell, facing execution. He knows he doesn't have much time left. He picks up a pen and smiles as he writes to Timothy, his son in the faith.

For I am already being poured out like a drink offering, and the time for my departure is near. I have fought the good

222

fight, I have finished the race, I have kept the faith. Now
there is in store for me the crown of righteousness, which the
Lord, the righteous Judge, will award to me on that day—
and not only to me, but also to all who have longed for his
appearing. (2 Tim. 4:6–8)

Paul looks back on his life and tells Timothy, "I've fought
the good fight and finished the race." He's celebrating at the
end of his life because the finish line is in sight.

It's not how you start but how you finish. The difference
is perseverance. Two athletes of equal ability join the same
college team, but one goes on to have a Hall of Fame career
while the other struggles, eventually drops out of school,
and ends up on the street.

Two entrepreneurs have similar investors and markets, but
one makes millions and the other goes bankrupt.

Two married couples begin with similar spiritual examples and families of origin, but thirty years later one couple
is happily married with grandchildren while the other is divorced and no longer on speaking terms.

What is it that separates the two models of success and
failure? There are a number of contributing factors. You hear
sports commentators speak of the "it factor." This quar-
terback or this point guard just has "it." Fine, but what is
"it"? Could it be confidence, charisma, competitive spirit?
Probably "it" varies for different people, but I suspect the
most important "it" factor of all is perseverance. Endurance,
determination, stick-to-itiveness.

Some have a bold, insistent spirit that refuses to give up.
He isn't overwhelmed by obstacles or intimidated by challenges. She has a confidence to keep believing and a courage

to keep going. When everyone is telling them to throw in the towel, they say, "One more round."

The magazine *Runner's World* told the story of Beth Anne DeCiantis. She was running to qualify for the Olympics in the marathon event. To make the Olympic trials, a female runner has to complete the 26.2 mile race in less than two hours and forty-five minutes.

Beth had a terrific start, but she began to struggle during the twenty-third mile. On the final straightaway, she was at 2:43 and had two minutes to complete and qualify. Then her foot came down unevenly, she stumbled, and she fell to the ground. For twenty seconds, she was down and dazed. The onlookers shouted encouragement. There was less than a minute left. She climbed to her feet and began to walk.

Five yards left, ten seconds remaining, and she fell for the second time. The crowd was shouting loudly now: "Get up! Get up!" As the final seconds ticked away, she crawled toward the line and stretched just across it on her hands and knees—three seconds within qualifying time.[1] She knew how to finish.

In his book *Adversity Quotient*, Paul Stoltz points out that for years, the predominant measure of potential was a person's IQ. But there are too many people with high IQs who are failures. He argues that there is something that predicts success much better than IQ, and that's AQ: Adversity Quotient. How much can a person endure?[2]

The person who simply refuses to quit has a high AQ. My dad likes to talk about leaders who have the head and the heart for leadership but not the shoulders for it. They have the knowledge and the passion but they buckle under the weight. They can't handle the adversity.

The good news, according to Paul Stoltz, is that while you can't do much to improve your IQ, you can dramatically improve your AQ. With God, you can strengthen and develop your ability to overcome adversity and persevere.

The writer of Hebrews addresses readers who are growing weary and losing heart. He challenges them to run with perseverance the race marked out before them. My friend who ran the Boston Marathon was telling me there's a hill in the race that has become rather infamous. The hill is known as "Heartbreak Hill."

After overcoming a number of hills, at mile nineteen, the runner comes to the longest and steepest hill in the Boston Marathon. That's the worst possible location for the highest hill—almost three quarters through, when a runner is reaching deep to gather the strength to finish strong.

You hear runners talk about "hitting the wall" in a long race. Lactic acid replaces the glycogen in the muscles. You know when that happens; you feel as if you won't survive one more step. Or so I've been told.* Even elite runners report that they hit the wall around mile eighteen. In the Boston Marathon, at that very place, the slope turns upward and Heartbreak Hill beckons.

I've heard other marathons have their own Heartbreak Hills. But they also exist in things other than literal running. Hearts are broken by those hills we fail to climb. We set goals, we give it our best, and we hit walls. Those are the moments that reveal our AQ. Sometimes the worst isn't the hill we failed to climb; it's the experience of finding out we don't have the endurance.

---

* To be as objective as possible, I try to learn from the experience of others. I feel this way about household chores too, but my wife differs.

In 2 Corinthians 4, Paul writes about the challenges and struggles of these moments. The Corinthians are running the race that has been marked out, but the hills are long, steep, and constant. Paul explains that the power they have is not from themselves; it's from God. They have endured because they run with his power.

> We are hard pressed on every side, but not crushed; perplexed, but not in despair; persecuted, but not abandoned; struck down, but not destroyed. (2 Cor. 4:8–9)

Here's how The Living Bible paraphrases verse 9: "We get knocked down, but we get up again and keep going." Paul is telling these Christians, "This is who we are. We are the people who get back up when we get knocked down." Running the race with perseverance requires us to have a defiant spirit that absolutely refuses to put a period where there should only be a comma. "The godly may trip seven times, but they will get up again. But one disaster is enough to overthrow the wicked" (Prov. 24:16 NLT).

What was it that kept Paul going? Why did he get back up every time he was knocked down? In the next chapter of 2 Corinthians, he gives an explanation for what motivated him to keep running the race that was marked out for him: "Christ's love compels us" (2 Cor. 5:14). *Compel* is a very strong verb—this powerful, controlling force. One of the ways you could define compel is: *can't stop, won't stop.* It takes strength and power to keep going, and the love of Christ has that strength. It's compelling.

I was thinking about that verse in my own life. As a pastor, when I feel tired and worn out, what is it that compels me to keep going? Sometimes, if I'm honest, I'd say guilt compels me. I know what I've done and said and thought. I know the mistakes I've made and the sins I've committed. Sometimes I let guilt and shame compel me, but in the end, I know it's guilt that knocks me down. It never helps me up.

Sometimes I let fear compel me. I do the right things for the wrong reasons. I'm compelled by the fear of what others think or the fear of failure. Fear is chasing me, so I start running. But I'm too consumed with what's chasing me to pay attention to where I'm going.

Paul says the love of Christ compels us. Please notice that it's not *our* love for Christ; it's the love *of* Christ that is so compelling. His love for me is so gripping that I can't stop and I won't stop, even if I could.

Remember how Hebrews 11:1 defined faith? It's being sure of what you hope for and certain of what you cannot see. The challenge is to keep the faith when all you can see in front of you is Heartbreak Hill. Anyone can run downhill, short distances, the wind at our back. But what happens when the road tilts upward, the sun beats down, we're exhausted, and our strength runs out? In life, the love of Christ, when we truly understand it, when we personally experience it, compels us. It won't allow us to quit.

Celebration

Paul says he has fought the fight and finished the race. It's been a difficult struggle, but he goes on to tell Timothy that a crown awaits him—a "crown of righteousness," as he calls it. Jesus will be there to fit it on his head, as he awards crowns to all the racers who have completed the course.

Paul is on the homestretch. He's celebrating because the struggle is real, but it's temporary and now it's almost over. Real celebration usually follows a season of struggle. In fact, the level of celebration often corresponds with the degree of the challenge. Your joy at reaching the mountaintop comes, in part, because the climb has been long and difficult.

Think about the moments of celebration in your life. Haven't most of them come after a time of persevering, of grinding it out? You wanted to quit but you didn't. You're able to celebrate because you kept going. You have a learning disability but you ace an exam. You haven't been treated fairly but you land the promotion. You've struggled with infertility but you find out you're expecting. You almost walked out but now you're celebrating your thirtieth anniversary. You battled your addiction but now you're ten years sober. The chemo and radiation were devastating but you finally hear the word *remission.*

We may have moments of celebration, but the ultimate celebration won't come until we get to heaven. That's where our hope lies. In 2 Corinthians, Paul reminds us why we shouldn't lose heart. He says that on the outside—that is, in the body—we're wasting away. Inwardly, however—in spirit—the process is reversed. We're growing more like Christ. We're being "renewed day by day" (2 Cor. 4:16). Withering on the outside, flourishing within.

The reason for that, he says, is that the troubles of the daily grind are toughening us, growing us up, bringing us closer to knowing what it's like to suffer as Jesus suffered. Eternal glory, he says, outweighs earthly struggle. "So we fix our eyes not on what is seen, but on what is unseen. For what is seen is temporary, but what is unseen is eternal" (v. 18).

Faith is being sure of what we can't see, and what we can't see is what's eternal. Heartbreak Hill might be all you can see; it's likely to block out the finish line. But this is temporary, and on the other side of that hill lies a reward.

When Paul describes what awaits us in heaven, he concludes that our current troubles are "light and momentary" (v. 17).

This is a man in fading health, nearly blind apparently, in the confinement of prison. He can't go to Spain or to other new mission fields as he wishes. Some of his friends have forgotten him. Some of his churches never seem to stop squabbling. He lives, by worldly standards, a lonely and frustrating existence. His future consists of the fact that soon his name will be called and an executioner will cut off his head.

And he's celebrating. His words ring with celebration.

Why? Because he knows that what awaits him is so spectacular that no mind can fathom it. All these things are light and momentary troubles by comparison. Don't sweat the small stuff. Among the final words Paul recorded, we read, "The Lord will rescue me from every evil attack and will bring me safely to his heavenly kingdom. To him be glory for ever and ever" (2 Tim. 4:18).

Christians die well; Paul went out singing, his hope in heaven so close he could taste it.

I've heard heaven described as oxygen for the human soul. When you're tired of running and feel out of breath, focus on heaven and be refreshed.

On the other side of Heartbreak Hill is your heavenly home. Keep running. Don't give up.

Fix Your Eyes

Other men would have seen a cruel execution. An injustice. A tragic ending. The pain of death. Paul saw a farewell party.

He saw himself on a ship disembarking for the farther shore, where something vastly beyond his deepest dreams would be fulfilled. He actually says this to Timothy: "The time for my departure is near" (v. 6). The word translated "departure" literally means "to set sail." Death was not something to fear. It wasn't the end. We've already seen that he expected a coronation.

A victorious Greek or Roman athlete was rewarded with a crown of leaves. But Paul is anticipating a crown that will not wither or fade. The word for crown that Paul uses is the same word to describe the crown of thorns Jesus wore on the cross. And when Jesus wore it, his very last word was *Talesti!* "It is finished!"

But that translation doesn't quite capture the fullness of what he meant. We can actually read it as a cry of defeat and miss the meaning. In his time, this was the word a soldier might shout in the streets after an incredible battle victory. The message was, "We're done, we've won—let the party begin!" He said this from a cross thrust into the top of the ultimate hill of heartbreak. He understood that beyond every Heartbreak Hill lies a point of eternal hope.

Let's look at Hebrews 12 one last time. The writer tells us to "[fix] our eyes on Jesus, the pioneer and perfecter of faith. For the joy set before him he endured the cross, scorning its shame, and sat down at the right hand of the throne of God" (Heb. 12:2).

Jesus endured the cross for the joy set before him. So, here's the question: What could that joy have been?

It must have been incredibly compelling. Think about what he endured—the physical, emotional, relational, and spiritual pain. The Lord laid on him the sin and guilt of us all. He endured all of that for the joy set before him.

What was it? It would seem to have been something worth coming to earth for, because it was coming here that placed him on that cross. What joy did Jesus come here for? What could possibly be worth the pain he endured?

I believe it was you and me. *We* were the joy set before him. There was no other way for us to be together in heaven, to be with him—so he endured the cross. For you and for me.

That kind of love compels me. Does it compel you?

That kind of love gives me energy when I think I have none left. It gets me going when the world seems to throw me into the dirt. It pulls me up and puts me back on track one more time. It renews my strength, helps me soar on wings like eagles, run and not grow weary, walk and not faint.

So I'm back in the race. Let the world do its worst. The love of Jesus is more than worth these light and momentary troubles.

Don't give up.

NOTES

Introduction

1. *New Oxford American Dictionary*, third ed. (2010), s.v. "encouragement."

Chapter 1 Keep Believing

1. Chris Tomlin, "How Great Is Our God," *Arriving* (sixsteps/Sparrow, 2004).
2. Larry Laudan, *The Book of Risks* (New York: Wiley, 1994).

Chapter 2 Keep Fighting

1. Hector Tobar, *Deep Down Dark* (New York: Farrar, Straus and Giroux, 2014).
2. Søren Kierkegaard, *This Sickness Unto Death* (New York: Penguin, 1989).
3. Gerald Sittser, *A Grace Disguised* (Grand Rapids: Zondervan, 2004), 33.

Chapter 3 Keep Perspective

1. James K. Glassman, "Whine, the Beloved Country!" *The American Enterprise*, June 2004, 48.
2. Malcolm Gladwell, *David and Goliath: Underdogs, Misfits, and the Art of Battling Giants* (New York: Little, Brown and Co., 2013).

Section 2 Throw Off the Weight

1. Alex Hutchinson, "How Much Does an Extra Pound Slow You Down?" *Runner's World*, June 7, 2017, https://www.runnersworld.com/nutrition

-weight-loss/a20856066/how-much-does-an-extra-pound-slow-you
-down/.

Chapter 4 Unhindered by Anxiety

1. Robert Leahy, *Anxiety Free: Unravel Your Fears before They Unravel You* (New York: Hay House, 2009), 4.
2. Leahy, *Anxiety Free*, 3, 4.
3. Sören Kierkegaard, *The Concept of Anxiety: A Simple Psychologically Orienting Deliberation on the Dogmatic Issue of Hereditary Sin*, ed. and trans. by Reidar Thomte (Princeton: Princeton University Press, 1980), 61.
4. Edward Hallowell, *Worry: Controlling It and Using It Wisely* (New York: Pantheon, 1997), 215.
5. Fred R. Shapiro, "Who Wrote the Serenity Prayer?" *The Chronicle Review* (April 28, 2014).
6. Scott Stossel, "Surviving Anxiety," *The Atlantic* (January/February 2014), https://www.theatlantic.com/magazine/archive/2014/01/surviving _anxiety/355741/.
7. Joseph Califano, *High Society: How Substance Abuse Ravages America and What to Do about It* (New York: PublicAffairs, 2007), 1–2.
8. Kyle Idleman, *Grace Is Greater* (Grand Rapids: Baker, 2017), 99.

Chapter 5 Unchained from Religion

1. "The Shawshank Redemption (2004) Quotes," IMDb.com, accessed September 21, 2018, https://www.imdb.com/title/tt0111161/quotes.

Chapter 7 Untangled from Unbelief

1. Philip Yancey, *Finding God in Unexpected Places* (Colorado Springs: Waterbrook, 2008), 179.

Chapter 9 One Step at a Time

1. Kaitlyn Tiffany, "Netflix Accuses Its Users of Watching 500 Million Hours of Adam Sandler Films," *The Verge*, April 17, 2017, https://www .theverge.com/2017/4/17/15331674/netflix-adam-sandler-movies-half a-billion-hours. Netflix users vehemently denied the charge through their attorney.

Chapter 10 Keep Your Confidence

1. Lewis Smedes, *Standing on the Promises* (Nashville: Thomas Nelson, 1998), 58.

2. Greg Miller, "Marathon Man Inspired by Wife's Suffering," *Preaching Today*, accessed September 21, 2018, https://www.preachingtoday.com/illustrations/2004/july/15441.html.

Epilogue

1. See Terry Fisher, "Persevering to the Finish Line," accessed September 24, 2018, *Preaching Today*, https://www.preachingtoday.com/illustrations/1998/april/2946.html.

2. Paul Stoltz, *Adversity Quotient: Turning Obstacles into Opportunities* (New York: Wiley & Sons, 1999), 6.

Kyle Idleman is senior pastor at Southeast Christian Church in Louisville, Kentucky, one of the ten largest churches in America, where he speaks to more than twenty-five thousand people each weekend. He is the bestselling and award-winning author of *Not a Fan* as well as *Grace Is Greater*, *Gods at War*, and *The End of Me*. He is a frequent speaker for national conventions and in influential churches across the country. Kyle and his wife, DesiRae, have four children and live on a farm, where he doesn't do any actual farming.

FAITH THAT GIVES YOU THE CONFIDENCE TO KEEP BELIEVING AND THE COURAGE TO KEEP GOING

RECEIVE 20% OFF YOUR PURCHASE OF *DON'T GIVE UP* RESOURCES

Use Coupon Code: DGU20

Get yours today at DontGiveUp.media

EXPERIENCE GRACE

connect with
KYLE

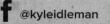 @kyleidleman   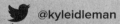 @kyleidleman

kyleidleman.com